REFLECTIONS ON A CULTURAL BRAND

connecting with lifestyles

REFLECTIONS ON
A CULTURAL BRAND

connecting with lifestyles

harvey hartman

The Hartman Group, Inc.
Bellevue, Washington

ISBN 1-929027-05-2
Cataloging in Publication data available upon request

Published by:

THE HARTMAN GROUP, INC.
1621 114th Avenue SE, #105
Bellevue, Washington 98004
Telephone: 425.452.0818
Fax: 425.452.9092
Email: info@hartman-group.com
Web site: www.hartman-group.com

This book is dedicated to
Cindy and Bryce Patrick

contents

preface

The exercise of writing this book has been an interesting journey. The idea actually came from several clients who prodded me and The Hartman Group team to become more involved in their branding process. As we began the quest to understand "brand," we wanted to be sure to emphasize two factors that we saw vacant in many of the other works we reviewed:

1. Our understanding of branding and "branding work" could not be "off the cuff," intuitive, or based upon a pedestrian consumer connection ("I've worked in marketing for twenty years, therefore…"). We naturally would not detour from our historical perspective. It had to be consumer driven, not through rhetoric but by an extension of our work built on years of consumer understanding. Therefore, this perspective could only be complete with insights on how consumers live, shop and buy.

2. We refused to create a simplistic solution to a complex challenge, one that historically has had terrible results with regard to the ratio of successful brands to the massive number introduced each year. We understood that the consumer is complex and the challenge needs more than your basic "10 Laws of Brand Success." We recognized that what we were setting forth was not to be perceived a "magic bullet"; rather, it was to be a process, a way of thinking, which clearly doesn't have all the answers. In fact, the real power in this text would be to create a framework for thinking, not a manual like all the "how to brand" books lining the shelves.

Our years incorporating innovative research from anthropologists, ethnographers and social scientists tied to our traditional methods has given us a robust perspective on today's consumer. The process of developing that perspective and the exercise of writing this text has proven to us that our "branding work" is a work in progress…as should be yours. The consumer/customer is your biggest asset and the definition of your brand—they use the brand, own the brand, live the brand. Because brands can be such an integral part of a person's lifestyle and because we know lifestyles are ever evolving, we need to be agile and ready to move with the consumer. A cultural brand is a powerful thing, but the power lies with the consumer.

We hope you recognize that the value of our perspective is in seeing it as an ongoing journey. With the development of tools and the framework for understanding the complex, fragmented and (often) contradictory human behavior of your customers, we only begin our quest. The success of this quest may very well lay in recognizing that all the answers are not here but may be found in the questions we raise along the way.

I hope you enjoy the journey (and what a trip it's been). As always, we would welcome your thoughts and ideas.

Harvey Hartman

acknowledgments

As always, the work at The Hartman Group is a collaborative effort. However, I would like to express my appreciation to a few individuals who helped make this book happen: Jack Whelan, Jarrett Paschel, Ph.D., David Moore, Ph.D., Michelle Barry, Ph.D., Jerry Savage and Joelle Chizmar. Thank you for your insight and continued vision, as well as your patience and support of my ongoing "ideas."

reflections on
the state of branding

it must be
an act of faith...

Here it is 2003—a good two to three years into the new millennium—and many in the business community (and beyond), remain wholly enraptured by the awe-inspiring power of something we call "the brand." At the surface, this fascination might seem understandable, for the artifacts and paraphernalia of this modern "cult" literally surround us as we go about our daily activities. Beyond the logos, the trademarks, the tag lines and the symbols that populate our bodies, our homes, our culture and our minds, we also see evidence of the tools themselves. The branding section at the local Barnes & Noble is literally collapsing from the weight of the vast number of interpretations and scriptures. Business cards representing professions as seemingly diverse as architecture, statistics, graphic design, law, engineering and advertising now proudly signify their clergy status with those two divine words "Brand Development." Finally, there are the "chosen ones," the exalted few whose divine genius is continually reified in our collective mythos. Imagine, if not for the supreme wisdom and insight of Phil Knight and the now infamous creative team at Wieden + Kennedy, we'd still be living in a world bereft of cryptic advertising, swooshy logos and garish athletic shoes.

And yet, in some ways this is all very hard to believe.

We operate in a climate, after all, with a new product/business failure rate that many experts place at well above 80%. And while we have yet to encounter any systematic investigations of change over time, anecdotal evidence suggests the current marketplace failure rate is no better than one would have encountered in the year 1903. Compared to other fields such as, say, aeronautical engineering or medicine—which have managed to improve airflight safety records and life expectancies substantially over the past 100 years— our best results often take the form of vague logos, abstract symbols, value propositions and so-called "mission statements," which profess to communicate our given product or company's values, emotions, beliefs and promises.

No wonder we continue to perish in such large numbers.

Factor in to this scenario the meteoric rise and fall of notorious brands from the now distant dot-com era, and it becomes all-the-more difficult to imagine our continued worship at the altar of the brand as anything *but* an act of blind faith; faith in a most unmerciful god, at that.

So we suggest the time has come to take a quiet step backward and reflect on the history and foundation of our modern preoccupation with the cult of the brand. Not so much because we believe such reflections will lead to the complete overhaul of a belief system, but because we feel the insight and knowledge gained from said efforts will allow us to more honestly and accurately understand what it is we are really doing when we say we are engaged in branding in the modern vernacular. Only then can we begin to (hopefully) make progress in our efforts to improve our branding practices, what we prefer to call "branding work."[1]

Similarly, lest this work takes the form of a religious jihad so common to business and economic circles— a sort of holy war in which the selling of one's own approach often comes at the complete denigration of another[2]—our approach here will be decidedly agnostic. Business analysts and consultants ourselves, we fully understand and believe in the felt need for strategic frameworks designed to increase the chances of marketplace success. And if some of those necessary constituent elements happen to be similar—if not precisely identical to—what one currently finds in the branding literature, then so be it. Our main difference here is that we seek to get analysts and marketers to such a position where they can make "reasoned, sound judgments" regarding their given orientation to marketplace activity, all the while remaining outside the ever-persuasive ideological grip of "cult of the brand."

Finally, once we've arrived at such a position, we will consider our own recent proprietary developments that seek to address specific analytical shortcomings in the current climate of marketing opinion.

---

[1] As a means of allowing us to a) critique typical approaches to branding while simultaneously proposing new ways to think about branding, and b) keeping in our general tone here of "demystifying" branding by putting forth a much more unpretentious, humble tone, one which by nature suggests the conventional ways of talking about branding are all marked by pretense and hollowness (a point many of our clients are now recognizing), I'm going to suggest the pragmatic label of "branding work" to all of the activities we formerly thought of as bundled together under the rubric of branding. Thus, part of effective "branding work" may include cultural branding, organizational fine tuning, etc. The "work" label stands in direct opposition to branding as a "science" and/or "art," both of which often seem more like magic and alchemy.

[2] A nice example here are the recent debates between PR and advertising as chronicled by the likes of Al and Laura Ries' in "The Fall of Advertising and the Rise of PR."

how did we get here, anyway?

As is the case for business and marketing, the story of branding is largely a story of control. Or, more accurately, a story of the anxiety-driven *struggle* for control.

Faced with the daunting challenge of releasing their products to a chaotic, turbulent marketplace populated by fickle consumers, those involved in the business of creating, manufacturing and selling products have always sought to wrestle back some sort of control over the whole messy situation.

And who can blame them? For after all, if we live in a world where we have the power to create machines that can craft rubber globules to exacting specifications before dyeing them any one of thousands of different hues, why shouldn't we believe that we can also apply those same energies and ingenuities toward getting a better handle on consumer interest in balloons?

The main problem, for reasons we will outline below, is that the latter goal (applying rational logics of science to the consumer marketplace for purposes of manipulating or negotiating the relationship between consumer and product/service) may well be impossible. For better or worse (and we say for better), people just don't behave in any sort of predictable fashion, and throwing the tools of science and rationality at the problem will likely only confuse matters, thus further distancing the consumer from the product, service or organization at hand.

Of course, this is *not* to suggest that one can not, or should not, ever think, plan or act strategically. Rather, we should merely be prepared to "come clean"—to be honest with ourselves and admit that we a) *have no business* maintaining such tight control over relationships with our customers, b) *never will* wield such control over said relationships, and c) are comfortable, instead, turning our attention towards what it is we do best.

Indeed, while the *search* for such control over the consumer relationship has pursued many directions and resulted in numerous developments in the marketing sciences—few with any long-term track record of success—it is likely the case that the "felt need for control," the impetus behind the search, is often the biggest hurdle to marketplace success. By extension, and at the risk of heading toward psychoanalytic parlance, we could suggest it is often the organization's "fear of letting go," that is precisely what may be holding it back.

a little bit of history...

If, as suggested above, the story of branding is a story of the struggle for control over market-based phenomenon, then the *evolution* of branding practices reflects that struggle as we transitioned from a produc-

Even though much of the contemporary consumer and marketing literature rests upon a view of the consumer as a rational, free-thinking individual, an ever-expanding body of evidence suggests most real-world behavior is anything but rational. So rather than continuing to "spin our wheels" in a vein attempt at portraying ourselves as something we are not ("all wise" and "all knowing"), why not suck up our collective pride and meet the enemy face to face? That is, since most of us readily admit that humans are imperfect, why not look to see if there are identifiable forces causing us to make mistakes in similar patterns and similar directions? From a marketing perspective, wouldn't it be darned interesting to know, for example, any potential scientific basis underlying our errors in perception and judgment?

To cite but one example on a rather cutting-edge front, a number of researchers are now taking a closer look at the cognitive limits to our ability to properly perceive pain and pleasure. These researchers are busy immersing human subjects in 39 degree water (supposedly quite painful!) in a variety of settings and durations and then asking these subjects to evaluate their relative levels of pain. Contrary to standard economic/business thinking, which assumes that individuals evaluate painful/pleasurable experiences (a nice day at Disneyland, a horrible movie, etc.) by "averaging out" their relative levels of pain/pleasure across the duration of the experience, these researchers are finding that humans look toward two primary measures (the level of pain/pleasure at the end of the experience and the relative change in pain/pleasure across the second half of the experience) in casting their evaluations. And while it may not be obvious at first glance, from a retail and marketing perspective these implications are really quite startling.

For example, if it is the level of pain/pleasure at the end of the experience that counts most, retailers may wish to seriously consider reengineering the "exit experience." Wal-Mart might be advised to move their infamous "greeters" to the exits. Similarly, big-box retailers such as Costco and Sam's Club may want to rethink the positioning of the "receipt cops" who hover conspicuously near the exits. Likewise, if consumers are, indeed, more sensitive to changes in pain/pleasure relative to an experienced standard, those retailers in the enviable position of commanding the highest price premiums (presumably by offering the best mix of products, services and experiences) may have the most to lose. Put another way, a retailer offering consistently average products and experiences might be looked upon more favorably by consumers than one that was originally far superior but had recently slipped—even if its current level was still superior to the "average" retailer.

Of course, these brief examples only hint at the enormous possibilities to come from what is a most exciting and (more or less) unprecedented development in the arena of human/consumer research. Namely, the decision to quit studying humans "as they should be" and, instead, look more closely at humans "as they really are."

by Jarrett Paschel, Ph.D.

tion to a consumer-driven economy over the past 120 years.

As the 19th Century drew to a close, manufacturers and producers of consumer goods remained focused on largely production-oriented issues. Enduring under the spell of the industrial revolution and its hallmark features—efficiency, precision, reliability and speed—manufacturers sought to outdistance their rivals by efficiently supplying products to the marketplace in a predictable, timely, cost-efficient fashion.

To the degree that such firms turned their attentions outward, toward the marketplace, to consider consumers and their needs or perceptions, they were mostly engaged in early, crude versions of what we now call "positioning." After first looking outward, to get a better sense of where they fit in the market, producers would return to the factory, seeking to refine or "tweak" specific products, typically by adding or subtracting features so as to be better received by the consumer. In short, efforts toward garnering control over the marketplace remained remarkably focused on production and manufacturing concerns. Accordingly, when advertising began to enter the fray as a serious marketing force (around the dawn of the 20th Century), we find it was often of an explanatory or educational nature. Compared to today's high-concept, abstract advertising campaigns, the print ads of the early 20th Century were devoted largely to explaining how the given product in question worked, operated or helped.

And lacking any semblance of the marketing sciences as we know them today, managers, directors and (often) owners of manufacturing firms undertook such market-oriented activity with a decidedly pragmatic, common-sense, "hands on" approach. In contrast to what one typically encounters in 2003 (i.e., the "VP of Brand Development," whose job it is to propose and implement intricate, channel-specific marketing plans across complex organizations with diffused layers of authority), those in charge of such matters at the dawn of the 20th Century were more likely to be "smart men acting in a reasonable and sensible manner to increase sales." And perhaps most important in that capacity was their ability to put common sense to practice, exerting direct control whenever possible.

the great consumer society

Fast forward 50-some years and one finds a remarkably different picture. The post-war economic boom of the '50s provided the finishing touches to what was now a fully realized, fully modern consumer society. Moreover, the evolution and development of this society can be attributed to several key intersecting threads and themes.

the birth of marketing as a discipline

The uniquely capitalist need for ever-expanding growth and profit caused manufacturers and producers to explore new and innovative methods of selling goods to the consumer public, and much of these efforts relied on newly developed social sciences of psychology, sociology and human relations.

While the natural sciences—especially chemistry, physics and engineering—had proven a wonderful resource for efficiently extracting every last bit of profit from production-related concerns during the industrial revolution, such intense focus on production efficiencies led to incredibly competitive marketplaces with razor-thin margins. As the "magic of efficiency" began to lose some of its luster, profit-hungry capitalists turned increasingly toward issues of scale, yet they did so from a decidedly consumer perspective. If science had proven a most profitable ally in the early days of manufacturing and distribution (extracting profits via efficiency), why not rely on it with equal confidence for the emerging challenges of the consumer economy (convincing people to buy stuff)?

At the same time, social scientists in the '20s, '30s and '40s—primarily psychologists, sociologists and anthropologists—were busy refining their tools and methods with all the fervor and excitement usually accompanying a discipline in its so-called "heyday." Anxious to put their new tools into practice, such academics made enthusiastic, willing partners for profit-driven business leaders eager to better understand specific commercial implications of the general question "what makes people tick?"

In this we see the birth of what would eventually become the marketing sciences, as business leaders began employing academic social scientists to address a variety of questions related to distinctly *consumer* concerns—consumer sentiment, taste, desire, attitudes, values, ways of life, etc. Finally, it is important to note here that by employing the "machinery of science" to systematically investigate and address important questions of the day, business leaders created an evolving discipline or practice—marketing—out of what was once "ordinary, pragmatic work by right-thinking men."

the transition from products and people to relationships

At the same time that business leaders—and, increasingly, practitioners and thinkers—began to look *away* from factories, machines and labor and refocus their attention *toward* the marketplace and the consumer, we note another subtle, yet equally significant, paradigm shift: Namely, we find experts beginning to look beyond the mere products and consumers themselves to consider, for the first time, the *relationships* between products and consumers. Compared to the previous epoch, in which consumers were seen as relying on products and services largely to fulfill basic needs, the hero of the great consumer society was seen as engaged in complex relationships with his/her goods. Some goods still fulfilled basic functions (water, gas, etc.), while others conveyed identification with certain "status groups" (clothes, records, etc.), and still others met needs for thrills and fun (custom-detailed sports cars). Moreover, the new-found interest in such relationships pushed well beyond the emerging marketing paradigm, to preoccupy the minds of intellects, writers, cultural analysts and others.[3] In short, we witnessed a collective revolution in thinking on such matters (consumption) that refocused attention beyond concrete objects and needs to include complexities of desire, identity and styles—all fragments of the consumer's overall way of living. In simple terms we could suggest this was the genesis of our collective preoccupation with what we now refer to as "lifestyle."

The importance of this shift can hardly be overstated, for with it came a new-found interest in psychosocial dynamics and issues of identity. If one wanted to shape consumer interest for purposes of selling more goods, one now needed to understand not just the surface-level needs and desires (food, shelter, transportation, etc.) or consumers' *underlying* needs and desires (security, comfort, intimacy, fear, etc.). As if that weren't enough, one need also take into account the innumerable relationships between individual needs and desires (on the one hand) and the larger spheres of social influence that regulated such desires (on the other).

And while it is certainly true that consumption practices have forever been linked to issues of identity and status (c.f., Veblen's 19th Century work on issues of conspicuous consumption), the difference in this epoch (~1940s forward) was the keen, self-reflective interest in such matters. By comparison to earlier eras in which, say, codes of dress were a straightforward (albeit often rigidly enforced) means of basic class identification, the denizens of the great consumer society became fascinated with the incredible detail and variation in possibilities for living. The 1940s, for example, saw the widespread introduction of "lifestyle" sections in many US newspapers and magazines, which allowed readers the opportunity to ruminate on the myriad of styles, fashions and taste predilections expressed by their neighbors and countrymen. And in a move that foreshadowed what was to come at the dawn of the 21st Century, some began to move beyond mere observation to, instead, ponder the ultimate meaning of our preoccupation with symbolic aspects of consumption.[4]

initial moves toward more diffused systems of control

This era also accompanied the rise of the large, vertically integrated firm sporting more complex, coordinated systems of control (i.e., bureaucracies). In stark contrast to the early days of the industrial revolution—wherein firms often specialized in doing a few things as efficiently as possible—firms in this epoch sought to expand by bringing as many activities as possible under the auspices of a single organization, in the process supposedly economizing on transaction costs and boosting revenues. Accordingly, we see here

---

[3] Among others, I refer interested readers here to the work of the French novelist and social critic Georges Perec, whose 1965 masterwork, *Things: A Story of the Sixties,* far predates our current fascination with lifestyle consumption.

[4] Again, I am referring here to Georges Perec's work, much of which sounds as if it could have been written shortly after the publication of David Brooks' *Bobo's in Paradise,* even though it was published some 40-odd years earlier.

the dawn of the multi-national conglomerates devoted to producing a wide variety of consumer goods (General Mills, Proctor & Gamble, etc.)

The important point to take away from this observation is that by comparison to earlier eras in the manufacturing and production of consumer goods, the systems of control in these scenarios were much more diffused and indirect. Whereas the factory owner or president of a consumer goods firm in the late 19th Century could often exact direct control over most aspects of the production process (design, quantities, schedules, etc.), the control over such matters in this era increasingly rested in complex chains of command spread across a number of positions within the organization.

summary

With the gradual evolution of our consumer society, generations of business leaders were busy laying the foundation for what we know now as the marketing industry. By comparison to their forefathers, who were able to simultaneously "look out toward the marketplace" while retaining enough control to enact change as they saw fit, change often based on old-fashioned common sense, the new marketers entertained much grander visions. By distancing themselves—physically as well as organizationally—from the daily grind of the factory and relying on the expertise of trained scientists to investigate the consumer in ever more exacting detail, marketers foresaw limitless possibilities for increased sales and revenue streams.

The main problem here, as we will soon observe when we consider the *current* state of our consumer society, is that marketers and business leaders were making the crucial mistake of implicitly treating the marketplace as if it were an "isolated research laboratory," a forum for scientific discovery much akin to that of the physicist's lab. Quite to the contrary, the marketplace is an ever-shifting, always-evolving social institution with considerable emergent tendencies, all of which make it a most unwelcome host to the sorts of inquiries marketers had in mind. Far from providing for more robust understandings of consumer behavior, the main result of all of the new-found forays into marketing—and the early precursors to what we now refer to as branding—was to foster the *illusion* of understanding, control and, ultimately, success. Businesses still failed at astonishing rates, most marketing and advertising campaigns hardly justified their existence, and new products still faced a daunting, uphill struggle. What was perhaps different is that business leaders and, increasingly, marketers *felt* "more in control" over that most disturbing of phenomenon—the consumer marketplace.

our current epoch

As we turn to consider our contemporary consumer landscape, we find that the themes and threads introduced above continued along their respective trajectories.

professionalization is complete

The professionalization of what was once everyday practice (i.e., leaders looking at the marketplace and making decisions) is now fully realized. We now enjoy the complex, mature discipline of marketing—replete with journals, literatures, schools, trade shows, conferences and jargon—all devoted to furthering our understanding of the consumer. And yet, as our discipline grows and becomes ever more specialized—as our graduate students devise complex new statistics, as new journals appear with increasingly specific subject matter, as cadres of experts arise to assist with what appear, at face value, to be the most basic of tasks (e.g., choosing a name)—one can't help but wonder about the end result of all of this work. That is, with all of our fancy methods, complex jargon, elaborate branding platforms and strategic briefs, are we really better off than we were 100 years ago?

Truth be told, we think much of this ambivalence is reflected in the preferred maxim of every right-thinking executive: "You know, when you get right down to it, branding is part art and part science…" Think about it, if the science part of the equation actually worked the way science is *supposed* to work—the way science keeps our airplanes in the air with astonishing frequency and our cars (more or less) running on a daily basis—we would have no use or place for the "art" part. After spending all of that time, money and effort with our science we would (presumably) be rewarded with reduced product failure rates and more reliable growth projections. Yet since we all know deep down that science part doesn't really work, at least not in the way science is usually thought to work, we hedge our bets by bringing the "art" part into the equation.

Moreover, while the "art" moniker could be invoked broadly to refer to all the nuanced insight and vision provided by the sum total of intellectual capital residing within the organization, we also know that too is rarely the case. Instead, the "art" is most often invoked by headstrong leaders as a way of accounting for what used to be "a wise man's judgment,"—as in "This is what I think is going on here…"

All told, it's our contention that when we hear that phrase, "Branding is part art and part science," the business leader in question is really saying, "I've been doing this long enough to trust my judgment, so I'm going to suggest we move forward with the following platform, and the science part (as anyone who has spent hours grinding away at a report only to see it used as a justification device for a previously determined decision can attest) sure does make me feel like we've got a handle on things and covered all our bases." Once again, science succeeds in a market setting by engendering the *feeling* or *illusion* of control.

HARTBEAT 1.2 our contentious relationship with jargon

— or —

"How our front-line team's desire to leverage mission-critical, low-hanging fruit for purposes of maximum channel penetration led us far astray for our original, actionable objectives."

Poking fun at business jargon is something of a sport among my colleagues. From my brother's comments after his first day of work in the business sector ("There sure is a whole lot of leveraging and fruit-picking going on") to our ongoing competition to see who can be the first to identify the "jargon du jour," we delight in our mocking wordplay. So I suppose it should likewise come as little surprise—what with the (fairly) recent cultural penchant for irony and such—that we are equally guilty of using these exact same words as we go about our daily work routines. Honestly, what marketer among us hasn't ever relied on the phrase "value-add," if only to make others in the room feel more comfortable?

Maybe the precise nature of this relationship is best evidenced by our continued fascination with the "jargon watch" columns found in the likes of <u>Wired</u>, <u>Red Herring</u> and such. As our eyes glance across the column, we scoff with disdain, while secretly peeking to find out whether we have been using any of the offending words in question. With any luck, the word has been part of our daily lexicon for well over a month, making us a bona-fide "insider."

So, why the seeming love/hate relationship?

As social theorists suggest, these areas of marked ambivalence—in this case characterized by the ritualized disapproval of commonplace behaviors—typically mask our collective discomfort with the underlying purpose(s) of the behavior or actions in question. Put most simply, afraid to acknowledge jargon's real purpose, we behave as we often do in such situations, we turn to humor. Of course, all of this begs the question, what are we really doing when we invoke jargon and is it really all that bad?

According to linguistic researchers, jargon typically fulfills one (or more) of four basic social purposes, the relevance of which vary according to the specific dynamics and goals of the group in question. Certain groups (chief among them criminal elements) seek to deliberately mislead and obstruct the rest of society (in general) and authority structures (in particular) through the use of specialized jargon and terminology. A hallmark of any criminal underworld is a subset of language understood only by the members of the given "gang." Likewise, given that most languages are necessarily imprecise, jargon also develops as a means of allowing members of a profession to communicate with much greater precision, though such use is often relegated to highly restrictive situations (the precision of legal wordings, engineering terminology, etc.)

More conventionally, some groups simply attempt to bolster their relative standing among the larger society through the use of such intricate, codified language—in the process (supposedly) according status to the specific sets of skills represented by the profession. Many of us have long suspected professions such as medicine and computer science were guilty of such tactics. Finally, at a most general level, we can suggest that groups invoke such specialized languages as a means of fostering a greater sense of unity and cohesion, drawing the membership closer together via shared meanings and experiences unavailable to those lacking the proper communicative tools (i.e., words).

In the uses of jargon outlined above, the one underlying theme linking all four is the notion of power and/or control. Whether for purposes of deception, for allowing professionals to "get things done," for status, or for solidarity—all invoke jargon as a means of concentrating and enhancing power. And yet of these four examples, only the second (allowing professionals to "get things done") is in any way related to objective, concrete, productive action. The rest all point, instead, to largely symbolic attempts at concentration of power.

Turning now to a business perspective (and generously assuming that business folk are not generally engaged in criminal activity), our attention focuses squarely on the last two purposes of jargon, those that we see as most in accord with modern marketing and management practice. To be sure, certain professionals such as tax attorneys or physicians may rely on jargon as a means of precise, effective communication when tackling highly complex or specified tasks, but such use hardly applies to business management or marketing circles. When we invoke jargon such as "low-hanging fruit," for example, we are referring not to a highly specified objective that allows us to accomplish a remarkably nuanced task. Ironically enough, we use the three word, 15-character expression as a shorthand for "easy." All of which suggests that what we are really accomplishing with our jargon is not higher productivity but, rather, the fostering of a greater sense of power and control, largely at the expense of those who may not happen to use our precise words to describe the contours of everyday life.

Maybe that, then, is the source of our ambivalence. That is, we so deride the very jargon we are all guilty of using on a regular basis, because we loathe to admit that our precious jargon is a largely symbolic attempt at wrestling control over what is, by nature, uncontrollable. Namely, the marketplace.

by Jarrett Paschel, Ph.D.

our continued, and at times perverse, relationship with relationships

The intense curiosity with the assorted relationships between consumers and their goods continues unabated, with recent expansion into ever more abstract realms including, but not limited to, lived experiences, social worlds, indigenous consuming communities and so-called "lifestyle tribes." Undoubtedly, the

Vibrant brands experience a kind of intimate relationship their consumers. But like any relationship, this partnership takes time, effort and patience. Just as nurtured relationships blossom and grow, ones that are ignored can fade and die. See if any of these sound familiar:

- "You don't understand me anymore."
- "There's someone else."
- "You don't work at the relationship like I do."
- "I've changed...I've grown."
- "The magic's gone."
- "There's just too much distance between us."
- "It's not you, it's me."
- "You're no fun anymore."
- "We don't talk anymore."
- "I still love you, I'm just not in love with you."

accompanying academic, cultural and scientific interest in relation-based theoretical perspectives variously described as network theory, chaos theory or complexity theory has likely reinforced such tendencies.

And yet, while analysts have been quick to criticize such preoccupations, frequently quipping that our obsession with relationships often comes at the expense of ignoring the basics at hand (i.e., providing real people with the things they need), we see such criticisms as secondary to the real challenges here. Namely, while our discipline begs us to examine all magnitude of complex lineages between individual people, goods and services (on the one hand) and higher order properties such as norms, values, trends, experiences, communities and cultures (on the other), the methods we use for such study are often sorely lacking. As it happens, the vast majority of our methods and models, influenced as they were by developments in economics and psychology, were devised primarily for the study of individual people (i.e., consumers). Questionnaires, survey instruments, scales, demographics, psychographics, etc. are all perfectly useful for measuring attributes of individual people, but unfortunately they do not work so well when applied to higher-order phenomenon such a experiences or trends.

Though recent advancements appear promising—measuring organizational performance (i.e., benchmarking), network-contingency analysis, contextual analysis and structural equation modeling (i.e., LISREL)—there remains much work to be done if we are to ever move forward with anything resembling a "scientific" study of consumer relationships.

ever more diffused systems of control

Finally, we note the trend toward increasingly diffused systems of control. And though it is certainly true that the hierarchical models of organizing so favored by large manufacturing and production firms have recently been shunned in favor of more flexibly aligned, loosely coupled plans for action, it is not obvious such tendencies have returned more control to those in charge. Marketing divisions seeking to exact more direct control over their customer relationships may have reduced the *absolute* levels of hierarchical author-

HARTBEAT 1.3 the trouble with case studies

Business analysts and writers are faced with a daunting problem. Like our brethren in the natural sciences, we are expected to provide accurate, compelling explanations for life in our little corner of the world (most frequently by explaining success or failure in the marketplace). Yet unlike our relatives in the natural sciences—who enjoy the benefits of working mostly in a vacuum (often a laboratory) with precise scope conditions predicated on a naturally occurring "order of the world"—we are not quite so fortunate. That is, while the "lucky" physicist retreats to the (relative) comfort of her laboratory to conduct carefully controlled experiments, we business folks must attempt to disentangle the cyclone of chaos that is the living, breathing marketplace.

And while it is theoretically possible to throw oneself into "the chaos," in pursuit of the most detailed, empirically grounded answers to our important questions, that pathway is plagued by its own set of challenges. Most notably, the low signal-to-noise ratio that accompanies such turbulence causes accurate information gathering to be both costly and time consuming. Put most simply, it's a royal pain in the behind to separate what is important from what is not.

As a result we are most often content to gather our data from afar. Perched high atop our analyst vantage point, we first make careful note of all the phenomenon, ideas, events, organizations, people and products that, for whatever reason, manage to rise to the top of the "cyclone of chaos"—a process akin to watching whitecaps roll in off the surf. Then, after (hopefully) careful analyses of these data points, we offer our insight and pronouncements in the form of what we refer to as a "case study."

Given the daunting task at hand (trying to explain successes and failures in the marketplace) case studies prove remarkably effective tools, both in their ability to provide comfort and reassurance as well as their power to illustrate key points and ideas. In one sense, case studies comfort by providing a deeper understanding of what is, by nature, unknowable. At the same time, case studies prove remarkably efficient when used to illustrate important ideas, especially as they play out in the vagaries of the marketplace. Just as the wise man, chief, cleric or shaman to come before him, the modern business analyst relies on the power of narrative to provide comfort, reassurance and understanding to those in need. It should come as little surprise, then, that the case study has become the de-facto standard explanatory device among business analysts.

The only problem is that despite all of its aforementioned strengths, the case study offers little in the way of explanatory power. That is, while we can rely on the case study to illustrate our ideas, offer insight into a "new way of thinking," or help us "see things more clearly," we can rarely, if ever, rely on the case study to rigorously explain success or failure in the marketplace. While there are a number of explanations as to this specific shortcoming, the most obvious and easily understood is the simple fact that in order to explain success or failure we need consider the sum total of all related cases.[1] Rather than merely looking at one successful example (the case in question) and extrapolating backwards, we need consider all relevant cases, successful or not, to come before it—and even then there is no guarantee we will have successfully highlighted relevant causal factors.[2]

And, of course, this requirement presents a significant problem when dealing with the enormous, turbulent marketplace, due in large part to the fact that we have no reliable means of cataloging failures. In fact, given the significant market failure rate for new products services and businesses, coupled with our woefully inadequate knowledge of such failures (honestly, how many of us can think beyond common archetypes such as New Coke, Bartles and James, and Orbitz—a far cry from what would be needed for explanatory purposes) the very idea that one could even begin to forge causal explanations with case studies seems downright ludicrous. Yet everywhere we turn in the analysts' domain, we see such transgressions with alarming regularity:

> Much of Kinko's success can be traced directly to Orfalea's unique business philosophy that was based on the founder's freethinking, creative style.

> Part of Williams-Sonoma's success comes from the fact that its fulfillment operation is in one place, Memphis…

We could go on, but we think you get the picture.

So the point of all of this is that we come clean and recognize case studies for their true potential. Used effectively, case studies engender a sense of comfort, familiarity and relief—assuaging our anxieties and fears of the unknowable—by serving as convenient illustrations and examples in our attempt to convey insight and make sense of the ever-changing, ever-so-turbulent marketplace. Conversely, case studies will never truly explain success or failure in the marketplace.

by Jarrett Paschel, Ph.D.

---

[1] In methodological parlance, we could say that the weakness of the case study method is that it is guilty of selecting on the dependent variable (i.e., trying to explain cancer incidence by looking only at patients diagnosed with cancer).

[2] It's precisely this sort of error that has plagued the medical sciences for years, the reification of "common sense" thinking by studying only those so afflicted. As we have only recently begun to reconsider many long-held "truths," through more costly double-blind studies involving non-afflicted patients, we can expect a "small avalanche" of common medical wisdom to fall by the wayside. To wit, last summer's crushing blows to HRT, mammograms and certain arthroscopic surgeries.

ity by outsourcing innumerable tasks formerly done "in house," yet such actions rarely concentrate power and control.

Quite to the contrary (and as anyone who has recently worked on a marketing or branding project of any size can attest), such moves result in tribes of experts (naming consultants, researchers, designers, branders, creative teams, PR firms, channel experts, and…), often dispersed throughout the country and with little experience working with each other, trying to come together to assist the client's efforts toward marketplace success.

So while organizations may be busy trying to regain some sense of agency and control by reducing hierarchy and emphasizing flexibility via loose-coupling, any potential gains are likely offset by the intense specialization and isolation that accompanies the push for expertise.

s u m m a r y

Looking at the chart below, we could suggest the story of branding has been the transition from a) firms reliably and humbly producing concrete products that meet perceived needs and are governed by a few interested parties working to the best of their abilities to b) high-concept firms with cadres of hired guns, seeking to establish long-term brand equity by building meaningful customer relationships and further reinforcing such relationships through the use of abstract logos and the staging of cutting-edge experiences. And re-reading that last sentence, one can't help but wonder if we have somehow lost our way, for we appear to have "evolved" to a world in which most—if not all—appear willing to sacrifice the predictability and (relative) comfort of traditional commerce for a few grandiose promises (who doesn't want to be the next Starbucks?) and the illusion of control.

mapping the evolutionary trajectory of key themes and threads

	1903	1945	2003

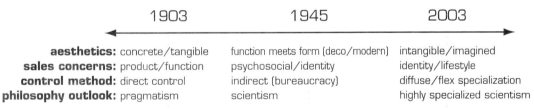

	1903	1945	2003
aesthetics:	concrete/tangible	function meets form (deco/modern)	intangible/imagined
sales concerns:	product/function	psychosocial/identity	identity/lifestyle
control method:	direct control	indirect (bureaucracy)	diffuse/flex specialization
philosophy outlook:	pragmatism	scientism	highly specialized scientism

Or maybe another way of putting all of this is to recognize how uncomfortable we all are (myself included) when we "come clean" and admit to ourselves that most of us can frequently be found parroting some version of option #b (above) on an all-too-regular basis.

Stepping back down from our soapbox, our primary criticisms of the cult of the brand are four-fold.

1. ## unwavering focus on relationships

   There has simply been far, far too much emphasis on the study of—and attempts to modify or manipulate—consumer relationships. To be certain, relationships *are* important and they do matter, but the vast majority of work to "understand, build and manipulate" such relationships is sorely misguided. Most specifically, many make the common mistake of assuming consumers desire meaningful relationships structured around largely utilitarian goods and services.

   How many of us have experienced the recent frustration of dealing with customer service representatives over the phone wherein the bulk of the conversation is devoted not to our specific inquiries, problems or needs but, instead, to discussions of the customer service we were—or were not—provided? Just last week my dinner was interrupted by a call from AT&T to inquire as to whether the change of long-distance order I had placed the previous day had "exceeded my customer service expectations." So much for building long-lasting relationships. We could go on with the infamous car-buying experience, but we think you get the point.[5]

   Alas all is not lost, for relationships do matter, especially with regard to products, services or experiences that are consumed in a more specific social setting. That is, as we move from goods consumed for basic, utilitarian purposes to consumption in a social context, it is worth trying to get a better handle on the consumer, the good or service, and the assorted relationships governing all. The important point, then, is moderation—to be able to recognize the perhaps important, but also at times limited, role relationships play in successful market strategizing.

2. ## problematic levels of analysis

   If we wish to take seriously these larger issues central to branding activities—lifestyle elements, relationships to social communities, symbols, iconography, etc.—we must frame our investigations so as to include proper levels of analysis. Despite what the best scientists, MBAs or PhDs may believe, instructing consumers to answer questions on a survey will never allow us to properly understand the meaning of a given product or service in a social setting. If one desires to really get a handle on where one's product or service fits in to a larger marketplace,

---

[5] "So, you are going to be getting a form in the mail from Honda of America asking you to rate my customer service, and it is important that I receive a mark of 'exceeded expectations' in every category, so if we can take 10 minutes to go over this now…"

one should be prepared to consider all manner of relevant factors (e.g., norms, values, communities, organizations, culture, etc.) each of which may operate at an altogether distinct level (individual, group, community, society) and may require unique tools for proper study.

3. branding should never be a discipline

We urge caution with the use of branding experts and, more importantly, expert information. If we were to be really honest with ourselves, we'd admit that much of the traditional activities we engage in with respect to branding—studying attitudes, creating propositions, building mission statements, etc.—are less about affecting consumer behavior than they are providing us with some much needed solace in the face of a most unpredictable, unforgiving, poorly understood marketplace. Ironically, the end result of such activities is often to distance marketers even further from the consumer.

Put most simply, branding is *not* a science, there is no magic solution and no silver bullet. If there were, do you think branding consultants would really waste their time helping *others* build successful brands?

4. resist the urge to control

Regrettably, much of branding is implicitly concerned with how to modify, manipulate or otherwise control the consumer relationship. Such concern might be warranted, or even useful, if not for one very important caveat—the consumer is inherently irrational. Prone to fits of unpredictable, spontaneous behavior (especially in the marketplace), the consumer makes a poor target for such energies.

reflections on...

...the customer as asset

Obviously, talking with customers (and consumers in general) can tell a lot about how a brand is perceived and how it fits into people's lives, but customers are more than just informants. They often become a part of the brand itself. Put a little differently, we are what we eat, drink, wear, drive, love, etc. It is no accident that branding has turned into the quest to insinuate reputations and status in the guise of products or services.

Some might object to what appears to be a conspiratorial undertone in this assertion, but the claim merely recognizes that most basic of human qualities, with apologies to John Donne, that no consumer is an island. From at least the 17th Century, apparently, consumers really have not been the self-interested individuals that we enjoy illustrating in marketing texts. Granted, viewing people as independent souls has certainly eased the job of aggregating their purported behaviors into pie charts. But how we limit ourselves for the sake of statistics and spreadsheets should not force us to abandon critical thinking altogether. In particular, we might spend less time thinking about individual consumer attitudes and behaviors and more time thinking about how "consumption networks" operate and how we can use them to build brand awareness, brand loyalty and bottom lines.

To start with, we need to appreciate the fact that consumption networks like any social network have properties or qualities that go beyond summing up the attributes of the individuals involved. This is where rugged individualism gives way to groupthink, peer pressure and related phenomena. For example, we all know that people do not always select products strictly for their utilitarian value. Status and other emotional concerns often dictate how and what consumers choose to purchase. How others perceive us matters because we live in a web of social relations that shape and give meaning to our lives. As a human activity, consumption is no different from any other. This is why consumption networks are important and why we should be thinking about network marketing.

When we hear the term "network marketing," most of us immediately think of multi-level marketing. Then it is only a small step from MLMs to images of seedy little boiler rooms, pyramid schemes and poor old Mr. Ponzi living it up with the Feds. At the same time, many of us cannot help but think about the vast sums of money just waiting for us if we could only be morally bankrupt for a little while. Okay, that takes us a little too far afield. The point is that we can all learn something from legitimate and illegitimate operations that exploit the power of networks. To keep us focused, note that the value of a consumption network resides in its ability to influence a large number of people quickly and automatically. Whatever hierarchy exists in the network is of purely secondary importance, because the goal is not to recruit "downlines" and reward those at the top of the Christmas tree. Rather, we want to concentrate on the efficient circulation of information and values that a network provides.

What we want to think about here are two elements of these systems that our conscience does not red flag and that are key to their success. First, something is necessary to spread enthusiasm for the network. Unless we can drive the growth of the network, it will not accomplish all of the wonderful marketing magic that we witness in multi-level networks. Avarice is only one incentive, albeit one that works like gangbusters, to induce people to join a network. For consumption networks, however, a primary motive is to share in the discovery of products and services that reflect the values that emerge from participation in the network. Prime examples of emergent values can be found in various social movements, such as those that gave rise to the current interest in organics or "slow food." In general, ensuring that our products and services have intrinsic value to a network gets us out of the trap of relying on simple greed.

The second crucial element to successful networks is their ability to get participants to invest in the network. By giving them a vested interest in the network we can help guarantee their future commitment to it. MLMs and the other schemes offer the promise of future riches to tie people into their networks, and we can make use of an analogous mechanism for ours. Again, we want to get away from reliance on any of the deadly sins, so direct pecuniary advantage cannot play a significant part. In fact, what we have in mind is better anyway. It is what social scientists call "generalized exchange," and it works like this: I will give you something today without anticipation of ever receiving anything in return from you, if I can expect my reward to come from someone else (in our network) at some other time. In a consumption network, this indirect give and take serves the same function as the MLMs' promise of fortunes.

Those of us mired in the economics of direct exchange relationships probably have a difficult time accepting that this sort of thing has any real impact. But it is the glue that holds modern societies together. We should not confuse the notion of generalized exchange with altruism. It is still a form of exchange or reciprocity. What makes it different, and special, is that it keeps the exchange open ended and in so doing, binds the affected parties together into a powerful chain of relationships. Direct exchanges, in contrast, sever rather than build links because the relationships between people last only as long as it takes to complete the transactions.

As a practical matter, we should always be on the lookout for opportunities to increase the participation of consumers in our brand's consumption network. Responsible efforts to tap into social networks in order to exercise the influence of customers over others are practically nonexistent, however. While many retailers and product manufacturers have some form of consumer outreach, which creates the potential for growing a loyal network of customers, the follow through on these programs generally ignores networking. As a rule, any worthwhile strategy for reaching new or marginal customers should be considered a candidate for marketing via social networks. For example, we could use the consumer reviews described above to encourage the generalized exchange of information through a network of consumption. The first step is simply realizing that customers are truly assets.

building
a cultural brand

introducing
a cultural brand...

A Cultural Brand. How to grasp the concept? We know what "cultural" means. We know what "brand" means? But put the two together, and you've got a concept that's both strange and, we believe, an important element in any company's marketing strategy toolbox. On the one hand, branding gives a product or company its identity. On the other, culture gives any social grouping its sense of identity. A cultural brand identifies and then enhances the link between group identities and product identities, and can often be a driving force in creating the very groups or subcultures that form their identities around a particular product or company.

In what follows we attempt in fairly broad strokes to describe our approach to cultural branding and branding work. This approach does not offer the answer but illustrates a way of thinking that is both innovative in addressing the marketplace and essential for understanding your consumers. The marketing task today differs from the task as it was understood in the mass market of the '50s and '60s because our culture is different. The most important difference is structural—the culture and its markets are simply no longer as homogeneous or static now as they were then. Sure, there's still Wal-Mart (in a category of their own, by the way) and other low-cost providers, and there will likely always be a place for the kind of strategies that they employ. But we don't think that's where the future opportunities lie.

Successful businesses of the future will need to understand that their success depends on strategies built on adapting to a dynamically changing culture and the changing definition of "value." What people buy is shaped by where they shop, and where they shop is shaped by how they live. We are also living through a period of significant cultural and lifestyle change, and while certain basic things remain the same, we should also expect that the world and how people adapt to it—what we understand to be culture—will look

cultural brands...

in retail...
- Whole Foods Market
- Anthropologie
- Trader Joe's
- REI
- Starbucks
- Krispy Kreme

in entertainment...
- ESPN's Sportscenter
- Oprah
- Grateful Dead

in manufacturing...
- Harley-Davidson
- Nike
- Apple Computers
- Luna Bar
- Odwalla
- Kashi

in categories...
- Organic products
- the SUV
- Bottled water

very different 15 and 20 years from now.

Until around 1975, marketers could look out at a largely homogenous culture shaped by the post-war economic boom. This is no longer the real world, and we're only just catching on. It begins with first accepting as a basic assumption that the dominant set of cultural values Americans experienced in the period preceding the social turmoil of the 1960s has fragmented into a wide variety of lifestyle subcultures[1] that in turn are reflected in a fragmented array of niche markets.

The market has fragmented because the culture has fragmented, and unless marketers understand the new logic of cultural fragmentation, they will not be able to effectively navigate the new lifestyle marketplace. People live increasingly complex lives in which they move among more than one and sometimes several of these subcultures, and how they think and behave while in one culture world is often very different from how they think and act while in another.

And so it's not as if any one lifestyle subculture tells us everything we need to know about any individual who might be influenced by it. Very few people live actively at the core of any given culture, but rather live lives in which they move in and out of several. And this obviously has an impact on how they shop and buy. Let's take a simple but fairly typical example: "Larry" might be the kind of guy who hangs out regularly Sunday afternoon with his couch-potato buddies watching football, drinking Budweiser and eating potato chips. But Thursday evenings he regularly gets together with his advertising agency colleagues and clients at a brew pub where everyone drinks microbrews and snacks on pistachios. Which "Larry" shows up in conventional market surveys? It probably depends on whether he's answering questions on a Thursday or a Sunday.

The essential point is that we have witnessed massive changes in the mass market as it existed in the 1950s and 1960s with the rise of a complex web of highly differentiated niche markets. For many consumers, if not most, this has created a culture and market context within which the way they live, shop and buy has

---

[1] Of course, there were always subcultures, but for the most part they were invisible or suppressed by the majority living in a mainstream culture they took for granted. The period since the '60s has seen the emergence of so many of these subcultures from the periphery of mainstream awareness to play roles that have a profound impact on how American society as a whole experiences itself.

HARTBEAT 2.1 the self of many selves

Our research has shown that traditional methods of market research are, at best, problematic. Most consumers don't fit into neat and tidy segments but rather have complex lifestyles that compel them to engage in patterns of consumption that are contradictory and difficult to predict. In a nutshell, our research has shown that consumer behavior is indeed "messy" and that the demographic of a given segment or population doesn't tell us anything about how consumers live, shop and buy.

Regardless of whether you've studied psychology or agree with what you've read, you probably have an intuitive understanding of Sigmund Freud's theory of psychoanalysis, or at least the angel and the devil battling it out on each shoulder. To illustrate, many of us can reflect on our days as children and recall watching cartoons in which the protagonist is faced with a dilemma. On one shoulder, an angel instructs them to do something good while on the other shoulder a little devil tells them to be deviant. At times, the protagonist's behavior is consistent with what the angel asks him to do, at others it's closer to what the devil instructs (and often more fun).

For many consumers, this internal conflict is compounded by the need to live and work in a variety of roles. Most of us can relate to the manager who has many roles, each of which has its own values, routines and patterns of consumption. Jane Consumer is not simply one consumer: She is Jane the Employee, Jane the Manager, Jane the Mom, Jane the Wife, Jane the Friend and so on. These contradictory roles and routines—and the conflict that results from competing needs and desires—sometimes results in contradictory and irrational behavior, which, in turn, makes it difficult for marketers and merchants to target consumer segments.

Consumers are moving targets, and it's conflict between the selves that causes the movement. When Jane goes shopping, the mother part of the self may tell her to buy organic produce for herself and her children, while the manager part of the self may tell her to buy sugar-coated cereal to help ensure that her child eats a quick breakfast that will allow her to get to work on time. Like the protagonist, Jane Consumer must negotiate this conflict between wellness and convenience. Similarly, each of one's various roles (e.g., manager, partner, consumer) may have different ways of interpreting products, brands and stores. In essence, each consumer is a self of many selves and, hence, should be viewed not as one consumer, but as many.

You reach consumers not by expecting them to act consistently in all areas of their life, but by understanding the logic of the lifestyle worlds where they live, shop and buy.

by Jerry Savage

become understandably confusing, making them unpredictable for marketers. Our approach accepts that this is the real world and proposes that marketers can begin to develop effective consumer-centered strategies *by not just focusing on the individual consumer*. While it may at first glance seem paradoxical, we'll attempt to clarify what we mean in what follows below. But it boils down to this: *If we want to understand the consumer, we need to understand that how she shops is determined by the rules that structure a particular lifestyle world and her experience while she's in it*. What she does when she leaves that lifestyle world might result in very different behaviors. We don't have to understand that; we need only to understand how she will behave while in a given lifestyle world.

It is therefore more important to understand the rules that govern the world than to understand the demographics or psychographics of a particular consumer or group of consumers. Businesses need to shift their thinking about how markets work if they are going to effectively adapt to this dynamically changing marketplace. It's no long about what are the psychographics of a particular consumer; it's about the psychographics of the world. It's no longer about how big the market is; it's about how big the world is. It's no longer about market share; it's about world share. Our "world perspective" is an effective tool in helping businesses to make these transitions.

getting beyond price, convenience & availability

Before describing this world perspective, it's helpful to provide some context by showing how three basic components have come to play an essential role in shaping value generation in the lifestyle-centered marketplace. One of these is the traditional PCA formula—price, convenience and availability—but two others, "lifestyle linkage" and "knowledge transfer," have emerged to play an equally and perhaps even more important role.

Traditional post-World War II models of retailing were typically designed to utilize some combination of the three key dimensions related to value generation: price, convenience and availability. As time passed, "selection" was eventually added to the equation. Even many specialty retailers of the era (jewelers, hi-fi shops, etc.) typically focused on some iteration of the PCA formula in an attempt to compete directly with more generalist retailers.

Our research, however, demonstrates that many of today's most successful retailers are not deriving significant benefits in terms of increased market share and/or price premiums from offering the most "stuff" at the lowest prices with a dollop of convenience thrown in. Instead, those achieving the most success are able to creatively bundle and manage key elements of three central components to meet the needs of a *specific segment of the marketplace*.

knowledge transfer

As part of the trend toward niche-market specialization, some consumers appear with increasing frequency to be seeking out retailers viewed as specialists or experts in their respective categories. As more and more consumers have access to specialized knowledge regarding all facets of modern life (e.g., via the Internet), retailers who are effectively able to both *communicate* as well as *demonstrate* this expert knowledge will be able to extract significant price premiums. In these scenarios, the specialized knowledge or expertise itself becomes a product.

While examples of such retailers often include those associated with "high-end luxury goods" (Porsche, Ferrari, Tiffany's, etc.), that need not always be the case. New York food purveyors Dean & Deluca, for example, have carved out a successful niche by relentlessly promoting their passion and knowledge of Italian flavors.

Likewise, this expert knowledge can rarely be effectively demonstrated and communicated merely through generic employee or consumer education programs. Instead, retailers must think creatively to bundle products and services in such a manner as to convince the educated consumer that they really do know their stuff.

Many famous jewelers and watchmakers, for example, build the retail environment around some stage of the production process, giving the consumer an open invitation to watch their expertise in action. Dean & Deluca spends much effort writing and zealously promoting its own line of cookbooks. Krispy Kreme has clearly tapped into this dimension allowing customers to watch the entire delicious process of mixing, frying and glazing their specialty doughnuts.

Finally, our research demonstrates that "authenticity" (a concept we'll explore more later when we describe the experience dimension as an element structuring a lifestyle world) is a significant dimension serving to organize and frame much of the knowledge transfer occurring in the marketplace.

lifestyle linkage

Clearly one of the most talked about success stories in the recent retail arena is the wide-scale proliferation of what we term "lifestyle retailers." By capitalizing on linkages to carefully constructed lifestyle images, experiences and markers, numerous retailers have managed to carve out a lucrative niche in the retail marketplace. Examples here include Pottery Barn, IKEA, REI, Restoration Hardware, Patagonia and Nike. In the grocery arena we could also place retailers such as Whole Foods Market, Central Market Foods, Trader Joe's and Wegman's in this category.

Here our research findings parallel those of Pine and Gilmore in their 1999 work, *The Experience Economy*. We find strong evidence that consumers are most likely to identify and connect with lifestyle retailers emphasizing *experiences* as opposed to those content merely to sell commodities in the traditional fashion, as might be typical of a Safeway or Rite-Aid. The foundation for lifestyle retailing and marketing rests on the ability of the consumer to feel connected to the people, images and markers that compose the associated lifestyle, and there is no better way to communicate those linkages than through living experiences. People might or might not need the stuff, but they participate for the experience.

By now, most folks are familiar with Niketown, perhaps the "granddaddy" of the second generation of experiential retailers. Central Market Foods, a retail grocery chain based in Texas, stages experiences by constructing an elaborate, circular, maze-like retail environment complete with individually themed departments (e.g., a produce section designed to mimic a functional farmer's market). IKEA also borrows on the maze theme, leading the home-furnishing consumer on a "journey through the world of affordable design," replete with free day care and affordable Swedish fare (conveniently located at the halfway mark of the shopping experience). Finally, Restoration Hardware chooses to divide their stores into "rooms": one enters in the "foyer," wanders through a "courtyard," and then strolls through the "kitchen" before heading to the "study" and "bedroom." According to Kellie Krug, director of marketing for the chain, "The store is arranged this way not only to feel like 'your home' but to give shoppers 'inspiration'."

price, convenience & availability

The third fundamental factor we find driving successful retailing is the emphasis on good old-fashioned price, convenience and availability—those familiar concepts that seemed most important to "traditional" models of retailing. Wal-Mart, Costco, Sam's Club, Home Depot and Lowe's are all examples of retailers who have achieved wide-scale success by capitalizing on these dimensions.

But the question here that has preoccupied analysts and consultants alike is: What is it that Wal-Mart and Costco are doing differently than J.C. Penney and Sears? That is, why is a newer generation of generalist retailers competing on price, convenience and availability replacing an older generation of retailers devoted primarily to the same organizing principles? A key is that one or both of the other two elements described above—knowledge transfer or lifestyle linkage—are a part of their retailing formula. Getting stuff cheaply will always be important, but the retailers who incorporate the expert knowledge and the lifestyle linkage dimensions will always have the edge.

Of course, this observation raises many larger and more fundamental issues. How can we begin to utilize the three central components to best meet the needs of our "target sector" in the marketplace? Or, on an even more basic level, how can we begin to visualize the marketplace to even know which sector we may wish to target? To address these questions, we have developed, as readers familiar with our work know, a model looking at the marketplace from a "world perspective." This is a methodological approach to understanding how consumers behave in culture "worlds" that we borrowed from the social sciences and that we think functions as a powerful tool to better understand where to find and how to market to the new lifestyle consumer.

reflections on...

...matters of taste

In the ongoing course of our work with marketers, manufacturers and branders of consumer food and beverage products, we are forced to grapple with the issue of taste. Yet whenever such issues and concerns arise—be they from our own internal opinions or, more importantly, the remarks of the consumers we study—there always seems to be a pronounced discomfort and uneasiness. In this, taste appears sort of like an unwelcome relative—the sort you're forced to acknowledge out of familial obligation, yet whom nobody really wants to deal with.

distinguishing between tastes

In many ways, I think much of the uneasiness and difficulty in dealing with "taste matters," stems from our tendency to conflate two vastly different, though ultimately related, notions of taste. I'm speaking here primarily of the difference between physical and moral ideations of taste. While the former refers to concrete, physical, sensorial taste perceptions (i.e., "The veal tastes salty."), the latter denotes socially located judgments of desirability (i.e., "I can't believe he would order veal!"). And while there is actually a profoundly interesting structural linkage between these two seemingly different notions, that remains a largely academic exercise to be dealt with in another venue.[1]

In this capacity, to understand consumer behavior and consumption issues, one flavor of taste plays an important, though often implicit and unexpressed, role. I'm thinking here of the above-noted "moral" expression of taste—a way of distinguishing "the good from the bad," "the beautiful from the ugly," "the refined from the vulgar," and so on. And I opt for the word "moral" here precisely because such distinctions are not absolute or "objective"—as if ordained by god, the natural world or any other outside forces. Instead, they are the product of shared knowledge, values and beliefs. And in this, we could suggest they are distinctly

---

[1] There remain certain perspective(s), variously described as "essentialist," "absolutist," and/or "romantic," which hold that many of the above distinctions (beauty, splendor, ugliness, etc.) are intuitively obvious, to all right-thinking creatures possessing sound mind and body and, accordingly, remain outside the scope of such moral relativism. Immanual Kant makes a similar case in his Metaphysics of Morals treatise. Personally, I find it useful to refer to this as the "Creature from Mars," argument—the idea that a creature from Mars, plucked down into our 21st Century, would be able to look around and see the same beauty we do in all sorts of styles, designs, patterns, etc.—because the "Mars" clause emphasizes the fact that such a position is ultimately untenable given our current empirical resources. That is, it is a philosophical conclusion and not an empirical reality. In short, while I'm prepared to entertain philosophical arguments from die-hard romanticists (ideally over a few beers), I like to stick to dealing with the answerable questions in my work.

social.[2] Finally, when conceiving of taste as the moral evaluation of distinctions, we can extend such evaluations to encompass not only attitudes and beliefs, but also practices and behaviors.

To cite a (hopefully) familiar example, there are certain "beliefs," "aesthetics," "rules of thumb" and "ways of thinking, orienting or behaving" that distinguish those at the core of the recreational-enthusiast world from those at the periphery, and the centralized expression of these proscriptions can be said to represent a "moral taste system." Or, in less-daunting language, we could refer to the "moral taste system" simply as a taste hierarchy.

From an analytical perspective, this taste hierarchy is crucial because it allows us to make sense of distinctions in things, as well as "ways of behaving and orienting," which are otherwise arbitrary or meaningless. One cannot, after all, logically argue that riding across pristine, backcountry trails on a loud, smoke-belching mini-bike is somehow more or less "fun" or "appropriate," than taking a quiet stroll along the same path, replete with a dignified respect for the natural ordering of the world.[3]

But by building a "sensory hierarchy" of the recreational enthusiast world—complete with the dimensions that order activity in such a world—we can begin to better understand how these differing perspectives build meaningful "fun" in sometimes radically different pathways. While "core" enthusiast may value authenticity, simplicity, tradition and/or history, the "peripheral" recreational enthusiast may garner just as much enjoyment out of dimensions such as technology, thrill, control and even destruction.

And while some may find the sense of arbitrariness in the above perspective—the refusal to judge one orientation as somehow "better" than another—a bit disconcerting, traditional approaches in economics, marketing and business, influenced as they are by a distinct, historical production-oriented bias, tend to view "reality," "things" and/or "knowledge" as concrete, absolute, real and immutable. Sure, consumer opinion may be subject to the "winds of change," (i.e., trends and fads), but at the end of the day, what matters in this mode of thought is a) what's inside the product, b) what's inside the consumer and, to a lesser extent, c) what's inside the competitor's

---

[2] For a nice perspective on the ever-shifting character of moral judgments, we could point to evolving ideas regarding sports stadiums. Remember that when the trend toward climate-controlled, indoor domes with artificial turf swept across America in the mid '70s, consumers loved those things. And even though we've spent the past 10 years systematically removing indoor domes and replacing them with another style, which seems "far superior" (the "retro-authentic" stadiums that remind us of our past), we should remember that those too are simply a style. In all likelihood, around the year 2020, we'll be hard at work building new sports stadiums to replace the "pale, insipid" structures we currently cherish.

[3] I'm referring here to anthropological studies of disgust: The literal study of what is/is not internally consumable (gustation/dis-gustation), how such matters vary by societal structure, and the symbolic extension of such norms to non-internal consumption practices (e.g., buying furniture at IKEA).

product. In short, this is a particularly absolutist position, which—construing consumers as having innate, concrete needs for products that have easily identifiable characteristics—seeks to connect the two in the marketplace.

A crucial and (hopefully) obvious difference in our approach is that we construe "knowledge," "things" and "reality," as an emergent property of social and economic life, as subject to a continual process of disputation, revision and adjustment among interested parties (read experience and community). And lest this spirit of relativism sound too much like the current wave of postmodernist thought that many suggest is paralyzing the sciences, I should add that one key difference between our perspective and those variously categorized as "post-modern," "critical theory" or—my personal fave—"post-colonial," is precisely that we treat the social world as subject to intense, careful, empirical scrutiny. Yes, the world and everything around us may be a so-called "social construction" in quotations, but those "social-constructions" are nonetheless very real, understandable objects of human work. Or, as I like to put it, while some post-modernists rely on a spirit of relativism to suggest "nothing matters because everything is a narrative," it's our contention that "everything matters" precisely because of the importance of said narratives.

getting beyond modernity

Taste and smell remain our most powerful sensorial tools. Simply put, nothing can evoke memories as powerfully as scents and flavors. At the same time, there is strong evidence that we in the West—as a people, society and culture—are finally moving "somewhere beyond modernism." For our purposes it is not important that we quibble about whether we are headed toward post-modernism, post-Fordism or whatever. What is important is that many—if not most—of us are coming to view rational modernity as simply a phase and not a permanent reality. And as our collective fascination with modernity wanes, as we begin to slowly shed our "rational" baggage and imagine alternative worlds and more authentic narratives, why should there not be a significant place for strongly developed, yet sorely underutilized, sense of taste and/or smell?

Think about it: The hallmark goods of the modern age were mostly packaged goods whose success was predicated on characteristics such as predictability, uniformity and efficiency—fundamental features of rational modernism. Likewise, advertising (a mostly visual medium) appeared the ideal source of support for such goods. Fast forward to our current epoch, and we find a consumer population that often shuns predictability, uniformity and efficiency to pursue authentic, community-driven experiences (decidedly pre-modern). And as most experts agree the best experiences are those that appeal to the entirety of the senses.

taste & design as a potential components of the cultural brand

It has always struck me that one of the shortcomings of branding in general is the ability to mediate or negotiate between the micro and macro. At the micro level, we can't ignore the fact that to some degree we are dealing with the relationship between people and things, and at least part of that relationship is concerned with internal, emotional dynamics. Flowing from a traditional production-centered logic (a throwback to when value equalled price, convenienc and availability), for many years these relationships preoccupied the minds of legions of classic branding theorists. And while we may decide they pale in importance when compared to the more macro-level processes addressed by our current perspective on the cultural brand, they still need to be dealt with.

These all important sensory mechanisms/experiences, then, may provide the ultimate linkage between the micro and macro—a way of mediating between internalized, individual understandings and the larger world that contextually bounds such understandings. Think about it, the world of design is so, so important because it serves as a means of embodying a set of aesthetic judgments (in our parlance a sensory hierarchy) into everyday lived practice and experience. To cite an example here, many suggest Apple's success has always been a triumph of design and not of technology or innovation. The design elements that made Apple computers famous (GUI, mouse, vibrant colors) embed a system of aesthetic judgments into the everyday experience of computer use. In short, design, and in essence taste, brokers the relationship between the internal and external, between individual people and the larger social world—replete with it's infinite complex of possibilities.

the world perspective...

One of the great truths of consumer behavior is that it is social behavior. We all belong to different groups—families, clubs, churches, schools, cliques, etc.—that influence us and are influenced by us in obvious ways. But social life also invades our personal lives in less obvious ways too. Large-scale trends and movements all tend to push us in particular directions, whether it's merely to go with the flow or to buck the tide. And even our daily routines take their cue from the neighborhoods, cities and regions in which we find ourselves.

How odd, then, that models of consumer behavior and the research methodologies derived from them should all but ignore the social context of that behavior. It's as if we could capture all of the relevant social influences by simply including more and better measures of individual characteristics. Unfortunately, we can't. What we can do, however, is incorporate features of the social context in our models and analyses in such a way that doesn't overload our conception of the individual consumer, yet allows us to portray consumer behavior more accurately than before.

This requires a fundamental shift in our thinking about consumers. Instead of treating consumers as largely autonomous decision makers, we suggest taking a look at the social forces that shape or give order to their decisions. In other words, view the "why" of choosing particular goods and services in the context of the activities in which they are used. Of course, common sense would advise us to consider how people use our products and services and to recognize that the level of interest from consumer to consumer reflects basic lifestyle differences. This hardly seems a radical notion. What is not so typical, however, is to use lifestyle as a device to characterize an entire world of activity, as opposed to individual consumer behavior, and to measure the intensity of participation in a particular world by all of the players in the relevant markets, be they manufacturers, retailers, distributors, consumers, etc.

Understanding the consumer as a participant in a *lifestyle world* also means refocusing how we market our products and services. While it is still necessary to devise and revise particular products or services to meet individual needs, we also must understand how our products and services find their place among the complex strands out of which a lifestyle world is woven. Understanding the context in which SUVs are driven, for instance, tells us that contrasting body panel colors is considerably more important to most consumers than low-end engine torque, despite the fact that the marketing success of SUVs depends on the fiction that we buy them for anything but mere looks. We could chalk this up to an irrational, lowbrow form of conspicuous consumption, but that would miss the point, which is to recast what appears irrational in terms of individual demographics or psychographics as something that starts to make sense within a world of activity.

understanding the world perspective

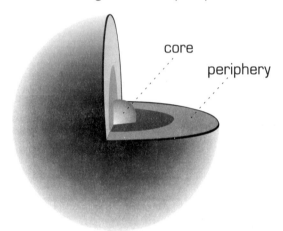

core

periphery

In what follows, we flesh out our notion of a "world," which we use as a tool to understand the rules of any of a number of different lifestyle subcultures—the wine world, the mountaineering world, the coffee world, the wellness world and so on. And as we will explain below, understanding how a world works leads to new possibilities for developing strategies to reach consumers who come into them.

The best way to understand how a world works is first to picture it as a globe. Within any given world of activity, we can envision a center or "core" as well as an outer edge or "periphery." The individuals and organizations in the core, even though they may not be large in number, are those most creatively active in a particular world of activity, while those at the periphery are those maintaining only minimal, infrequent and less-intense involvement in that world.

dimensions within worlds

As anyone who has ever encountered a wine aficionado or outdoor enthusiast knows, those at the center see things very differently from those at the edges. What to the ordinary person looks like a boot may actually be the state-of-the-art in outdoor climbing gear, boasting titanium shanks and weighing a remarkably lightweight 12 oz. Likewise, whereas most of us will see a glass of wine and think "red" or "cabernet," the wine geek wants to know about vintage and vinification techniques, or he might wonder if his 1994 Caymus Special Selection Cabernet will make a good match for a grilled beef tenderloin. What a consumer sees and what he cares about depends on where he is situated within a given world. The factors that determine what a customer sees or cares about we call "dimensions."

Just as we can speak of a dimension known as "customer satisfaction," along which individuals may be placed in a continuum ranging from low to high, so too we find dimensions that organize and affect some areas of a world more strongly than others. For example, in the world of wine we find several important dimensions, one of which is price. While price is very important for wine consumers located at the periphery, it is of minimal importance for those active at the core. Serious wine consumers care about other things. We are not suggesting that price is never an issue to those at the core; there are exceptions to every pattern. Rather, when looking at the world from an aggregate (not individual) perspective, price becomes an insignificant dimension at the core. Identifying, locating and understanding these dimensions is the first task for anybody who wants to truly understand how things work and how people tend to behave within a given world.

Let's look more carefully at the dimensions we developed to describe the rules governing the Wellness World. Our research in the wellness marketplace has led us to these particular dimension labels, but we've also found that these basic dimensions can be tailored with some small adjustments to almost any lifestyle-driven world. If you take, for instance, wine or extreme sports, each world has its hard-core fanatics and each has its dabblers, but they participate in the world on very different terms. Dabblers don't go comfortably into the core, but they may admire those who can function effectively there and seek to emulate them at least part of the time. And the world even at the periphery is profoundly influenced by the activity of the people at the core who are continuously innovating and driving developments within the world. Today's fashions at the periphery are often cheap knockoffs of something that is or was a genuinely innovative item at the core.

The "core" of a particular world is structured by two key dimensions: knowledge and authenticity. Individuals at the core are actively engaged in the pursuit of specialized knowledge about the products and services provided in this world, and they participate in this world not just because they want the stuff that's sold there, but because they live lives and engage in activities that require the "stuff" in order to function at the highest level within that world. The stuff is secondary to their expertise, and their exper-

dimensions of consumption organizing the world of "wellness"

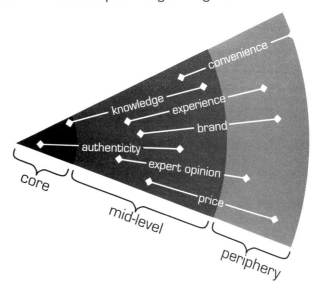

tise profoundly influences how and what kind of stuff sells from the core to the periphery of the world.

Once we have identified the dimensions that serve to order a given world of activity, we can even extend this knowledge and begin to think about where brands and products fall. Here, we offer a sketch of the Coffee World with respect to its specific brands and products:

Not surprisingly, we would expect to find at the center of the coffee world those products offered by artisan roasters that stress the authentic coffee experience, replete with a hefty dose of knowledge. In local neighborhoods up and down the West Coast—from San Francisco to Vancouver—one finds hundreds of small, artisan roasters often operating within the confines of a single coffee shop. In many instances, the roasting machine is located within the shop itself, inviting the customer to witness the "true art of the roast." Also in this location we might expect to find high-quality, "specialty" coffees often with a regional appeal (e.g., Torrefazione). Towards the middle of the coffee world, one finds folks like Starbucks and Seattle's Best, who rely on the retail experience as a conduit for branding a product associated with a lifestyle image. At one point early in Starbucks' history, it would have been located much closer to the core of the coffee world. However, now with the massive expansion across the country and worldwide, we see their mainstream appeal moving them farther out into the mid-level where the majority of the consumers reside. Finally, at the periphery, we would expect to find the likes of Folgers, Maxwell House or, in the retail sector, Dunkin Donuts, all branded products stressing convenience and price over lifestyle, experience, expert opinion or authenticity. Interestingly, in parts of New England, where Dunkin Donuts' coffee is revered for its simplicity and experience with long lines that are commonplace during the morning workweek rush, Dunkin Donuts' placement moves much farther into the mid-level of the world. While those in the core may appear a central area of concern for curious researchers (perhaps these are the individuals and organizations seen as driving trends and innovation), one should not lose sight of the larger world. After all, as their large numbers indicate, the bulk of the market resides in the mid-level.

It is the producers and retailers at the core, however, who are among the world's experts, whether they are connoisseurs in the coffee world, critics in the wine world or active expert participants in the world of extreme sports. The products and services they provide are developed to serve the needs and tastes identified by this vanguard. Our lightweight, titanium-shank hiking boot was developed to solve particular problems encountered by mountaineers who operate on the highest level of that sport, yet it's something that people who participate in the mid-level or periphery of the world can buy too. They may not really need it, but it makes them *bona fide* members of the world if they buy a pair and wear them. The point, though, is this: They don't want the boots; they want what the boots represent, which is membership in a lifestyle world even if they do not function at its core.

What will always distinguish core persons from others is their mastery, their proven expertise and knowledge. Their knowledge is something that comes from authentic experience in the real world and their authentic engagement with the products—not from a package label or an article in *Time* magazine. The people in the mid-level are either aspirants—they buy to emulate the people they wannabe and are hungry for knowledge about the product because it is part of their learning curve in their aspiration to be more like the masters at the core—or they are people who are satisfied to simply remain in the mid-level as knowledgeable fans. The people at the periphery are mostly clueless about that particular world and don't care to know anything about the product. They will buy a particular style of boot or running shoe because it has become trendy (everybody's wearing them) or because they are comfortable, but they aren't willing to pay the kind of prices people at the core or mid-level are.

This is a well-known phenomenon to marketers of luxury goods. People with lower status emulate those with higher status. "Status," however, is no longer a homogenous category. It's defined differently in different worlds. Our world model is designed to help product marketers and retailers to identify the world in which they must operate and then to identify the key dimensions that are influencing consumers within that world. Once that has been accomplished, the "branding work" can begin.

This is the basis we use in trying to understand a business's customers and for framing strategies for developing increased market profitability within a particular retailing or manufacturing sector. At its most useful, this model allows one to identify where consumption takes place in the world. This in turn gives retailers or consumer products manufacturers a framework in which to understand and more effectively reach consumers in their current customer base as well as any segment of the world into which they might wish to expand. While the dimensions can be adapted to the particularities of any world of activity, the three central components—knowledge transfer, lifestyle linkage and value generation—are fundamental elements in structuring the core, mid-level and periphery respectively. Price, convenience and availability structure the dimensions at the "periphery," while knowledge and authenticity structure the "core." At mid-level, the realm of the uncommitted or aspirant, lifestyle markers (images, symbols, icons, designs, etc.) and, to some degree, price are the more important dimensions.

where in the world are the people?

This world perspective doesn't require that we change significantly the way we go about gathering information; it's just a better way of representing what we find out. We're still out in the field talking to people, studying and observing everything that is going on. The difference now is that rather than worrying about explaining individual consumer behavior, we are more interested in explaining, in detail, the inner workings of various dimensions of the particular world in question. Of course, this raises a more fundamental question: How does a thorough understanding of a specific world of activity allow one to target a specified set of consumers?

Our model differs from traditional market segmentation models in that it focuses not on aggregating individual types according to similar attitudes or behaviors, but focusing on how these individual behaviors and attitudes are shaped by transpersonal or cultural influences. No individual operates in a vacuum, and everyone's attitudes and behaviors are profoundly influenced, consciously or unconsciously, by larger social factors. Our model helps us to understand how the individual consumer lives, where she shops and what she buys by understanding the higher-order worlds in which she participates.

Of course, these worlds are populated by living, breathing individuals. And if you were to look at how they behave over the course of a week or a month, you would find that they behave in ways that often appear unpredictable and individualized. But when they enter a given world, those behaviors are more predictable according to the dimensions that define the part of the world in which they happen to be. That's the point of focusing more on the worlds in which people participate than on individual attributes. We don't necessarily require an individual to exhibit totally consistent attitudes and behaviors when looking at their lives as a whole, but there is a manageable consistency when looking at how they behave within a given region of a lifestyle world.

As our hypothetical consumer, Larry, illustrated earlier, in a complex society such as ours, it's not unusual for someone who has one set of interests also to have another—he's a Bud guy on the weekends but a microbrew guy when he's with work colleagues and clients. To expect an individual to behave consistently in all the different worlds in which he might enter, betrays a naïve understanding of how most people live today. What's important is not to impose artificial consistency on consumer segments in a misguided effort to "target" them, but to understand what is going on in a world that would influence any individual to want to purchase a particular product. Or, to put it the other way around, what role does a particular product play in the various worlds in which a consumer moves? This means understanding which dimensions of a particular world are likely to have the most impact on a given consumer's buying decisions on the one hand, and on the other, understanding what product attributes resonate with these dimensions.

Let's look at three examples of consumer behavior. The figure to the right highlights where three different consumers fall on the core to periphery scale. Each exemplifies a different lifestyle and lifestyle behaviors using the Wellness World as an example:

jeff, periphery wellness consumer

- Often substitutes snacks for meals, trying to keep it "healthy" (SnackWell's)
- Runs three times a week
- Smokes a pack a day, claiming he's "trying to quit"
- Does all his shopping at the neighborhood Safeway…and, of course, 7-Eleven
- Takes vitamin C when he's sick

amanda, mid-level wellness consumer

- Nearing menopause, Amanda recently spent time learning about the health benefits of soy
- Tries to eat healthy as much as possible, though she admits she doesn't like to splurge on organic produce
- Wishes she exercised more
- Learns a lot about herbal supplements from friends, co-workers (but still isn't taking them)

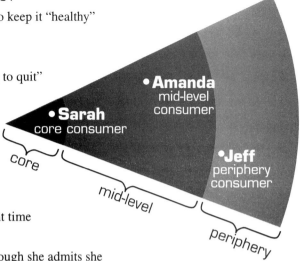

sarah, core wellness consumer

- Uses strictly organic produce, worrying about the certification process of each
- Practices Yoga regularly, but first researches the qualifications of her instructor
- Takes only natural vitamin E from "her" brand
- Buys only cruelty-free personal care products

Beyond being able to describe and characterize the organization of an entire world of activity, our model enables us to accomplish three other important tasks to identify:

1. the relative distribution of the consumer population within that world,
2. key areas of market opportunity, and
3. the opportunity to create your own world.

So, the world model allows us to look not solely at the individual but also takes into account the broader social-historical context within which he or she is situated. And we have suggested that this type of approach puts one in a better position to identify and capitalize upon opportunities in the market.

reflections on...

...market research

Market research is not rocket science. It is actually much more complicated. And the fact that most market researchers would not know a double integral from a partial derivative is one of the great ironies of the profession. Don't get me wrong. I truly do not believe an advanced calculus text will unlock all the mysteries of the consumer universe, but perhaps a more rigorous conceptualization of consumer behavior could help us deal with a few pesky complications that seem to get in the way of branding work.

Now, I do not claim any special knowledge of fluid mechanics or thermodynamics, but I'm fairly certain that modern rocket design no longer tries to mimic the flight of birds. Yet, in market research we naively cling to a simplistic notion of human behavior to set into motion something much more unpredictable than any machine. The model of the consumer that informs most current market research fails to do justice to reality in at least three fundamental areas. First, it seems to think individuals float about in a social vacuum. Second, it mechanically ties consumer behavior to consumer attitudes. Third, it is oblivious to inconsistencies and contradictions in individual behavior. Let's examine each of these in turn.

consumer-level research

Historically, economists and psychologists have dominated the study of consumer behavior. And their preoccupation with the abstract individual continues to set the standard for research. Unfortunately, modern developments in these two fields, which have struggled to treat individuals less, well, individually, seem to have gone unnoticed by the vast majority of market researchers. For example, a simple exchange relationship between only two people creates such a range of possible outcomes (from jointly beneficial to unilaterally beneficial to jointly harmful) that it is virtually impossible to predict the outcome. And when the two people don't have any reason to trust one another they are as likely to just walk away as they are to buy and sell. If we blissfully ignore the fact that something is going on between individuals that did not exist in the vacuum of the traditional behavioral model, we might end up pitting our brand strategies against the emotional by-products of social interaction, such as mistrust, anxiety, fear, etc.

A second weakness of the model of consumer behavior handed down by economists and their brethren from psychology is its inadequate treatment of the relationship between an individual's attitudes and behaviors. In this model, behavior flows from attitudes, possibly with some slippage, in a very rational and straightforward manner. Apparently, we cannot quite shake the belief that consumers act merely on their convictions, despite the large and growing body of evidence to the contrary. We continue to see, for example, dubious attempts to uncover consumer need gaps and market opportunities using the latest in psychographics, as if simply matching consumer needs to product benefits is the formula for success. Does anyone honestly believe this formula explains the ascendancy of the SUV over the minivan, or the dramatic rise of the Starbucks and Nike brands? No doubt, there are success stories that demonstrate the value of identifying and meeting pent up consumer needs, such as getting whites even whiter, but I suspect these describe the commoditization of products better than they describe strong brands.

The third area that could use a reality check is more or less responsible for the idea that once you "understand" consumers you can select and target the right ones. Most marketing and advertising campaigns choose a relatively well-defined "target" audience in order to channel their resources effectively and craft appropriate consumer-oriented messages. Unfortunately, real consumers rarely justify such a uniform approach to marketing. Who among us has not been part of a target segment on one occasion only to exit on the next occasion? This should tell us something significant about how we define our targets. For one thing, it suggests that whole consumers may not be the best targets. In the normal course of events, circumstances and demands pull us in different directions, which we manage by wearing different hats and compartmentalizing our lives. So, the environmentalist who drives his "green" hybrid to work every day can still burn weekend rubber flogging his other sports car around the local racetrack. This consumer would easily score near the top of the LOHAS pyramid and yet many of his fellow "Cultural Creatives" would probably be horrified by his weekend exploits. The key to understanding normal consumer behavior like this lies in recognizing that the true target is fleeting and occasion-based, not an internally consistent individual whose behavior reflects a well-defined value system.

occasion-level research

Although the market researcher's consumer appears a shallow imitation of the true consumer, the magnitude of the differences between them suggests how we might sketch out an alternative to the fiction currently in use. This alternative, however, is not a new and improved model of the consumer. Just as we would not want to waste time perfecting a giant model bird in order to fly to the moon, it is not necessarily worthwhile improving the consumer model for purposes of branding. Instead, we suggest taking a slightly different approach, one that builds on the existing consumer model while avoiding the three problem areas described above. It achieves all this by shifting the focus from individuals to individual acts. By going to a more granular level than the individual, we can easily avoid the issue of inconsistent attitudes or behaviors because there is no requirement that an individual act be consistent with another individual act. Moreover, using acts draws attention to the circumstances that condition each individual act and is not overly reliant on the rationality that supposedly links particular attitudes to specific behaviors. Finally, this activity-oriented approach easily accommodates properties of social relationships as an integral dimension.

One obvious reaction to treating acts or activities as subjects for study is that we cannot easily count the acting individuals and, consequently, cannot readily "size" an opportunity or market in the usual sense. This will doubtless concern some marketing types who need household penetration or individual incidence figures for reports that no one ever reads. In fact, however, it is possible to estimate these numbers, but we have to wonder why, given our reservations about treating people as meaningful wholes from a market research perspective. Arguably more valuable are the analogous expressions calculated at the occasion level, since these give a more representative picture of how consumption actually takes place. In particular, analyzing occasions rather than individuals tells us directly how the level of consumption varies by any number of salient attributes. Note, especially, that nothing prevents individual characteristics, such as demographics and psychographics, from being characteristics of a particular consumption occasion. We can go further, there is nothing to prevent us from combining all of the characteristics of the individuals taking part in the occasion as a contextual measure that gets at the interaction by-products of each social situation.

A final comment with regard to analyzing activities on an occasion-by-occasion level is in order. We have argued that it is difficult—if not pointless—to target and segment individual consumers, because consumers do not fit neatly into the boxes we create. In part, this reflects the simplifying limitations of the methodology that generates the boxes, but, more importantly, it is a result of the fact that the individual-level model is inappropriate for understanding most consumer behavior. Rather, we should examine the conditions under which any consumer becomes a potential target and focus on those conditions. Learning how to market to occasions is ultimately where we need to put our branding energy. And here is a marketing hint, instead of worrying about what "your consumer" looks like, think of ways to insinuate your brand into the situations and occasions that best suit your products and services. If you handle this correctly, your consumer will find you.

elements of
a cultural brand…

Understanding how our world perspective works lays the foundation for the next phase, which is to understand how a cultural brand develops. Our model gives us the basic tool insofar as it helps us to articulate the actions of consumers with the institutions, organizations, manufacturers, retailers, etc. who make up a given lifestyle world. And the dovetailing of all these players is what enables us to see clearly how products and services are transformed from mere stuff into a cultural brand.

If a brand is "cultural," it plays an identity-defining role for people who use it. This phenomenon is similar to what is already well known in the designer clothing world where clothing articles often ostentatiously display their brand. Nike, Tommy Hilfiger, Donna Karan, Ralph Lauren, Abercrombie & Fitch have been among the most successful in this kind of identity branding in the apparel industry. But a cultural brand requires more than a well-recognized name or logo. It must also incorporate some form of brand community, with activities and language organized about the brand, and it must give expression to its "identity" through non-trivial experiences rooted in a social context.

Now, you can look at a particular world and ask yourself where every established brand fits as a first step toward understanding and building a cultural brand. We could use the world perspective to map out the fashion world, for instance, and we could place different designers or brands in spaces within that world depending on whether they fit more readily into the core (designers of high couture), or the core/mid-level (Armani, Versace), mid-level/periphery (Ralph Lauren, Donna Karan), or at the periphery (Mossimo/ Target).

But where does a brand such as Patagonia fit? Patagonia is significant, not as a particularly strong brand in the world of fashion, but because it solidified its position in that world and in the larger world of apparel by cultivating many of the elements of a cultural brand. In a sense, Patagonia created its own world by locating itself (i.e., actively participating) in several worlds simultaneously. Brands relevant to one world often play a more significant role in other lifestyle worlds—such as those structured around outdoor or environmentally conscious activities. Patagonia's early roots in the world of technical high-altitude sports gave it instant credibility among hard-core outdoors enthusiasts, which it parlayed into a successful sports apparel/outfitter business. The Patagonia cachet now appeals to a large cross-section of well-heeled consumers attracted to its earth-friendly stance and sporty styles. By wearing their gear, consumers participate in the aspirational lifestyle that Patagonia represents. As Patagonia writes on their web site:

> We prefer the human scale to the corporate, vagabonding to tourism, the quirky and lively to the toned down and flattened out. We used to call our own world of alpinists and surfers a dirtbag culture: of temp jobs and long summers; of foraged meals and tribal travel that followed the seasons, from summer climbs in Yosemite to Baja's winter surfbreaks to spring kayaking. And if many of us now work more than we climb, and care more for our families than for bumming about, we still sound our appeal to the dirtbag within, the need for the wild dirtbag spirit to survive in our e'd-out culture.

Is Patagonia a mover and shaker in the fashion world? Not exactly. Is it a solid cultural brand with an ever-expanding customer base? Just ask a loyal "dirtbag" and the answer will be a resounding, "Yes!"

So, from our perspective, a cultural brand can successfully appear in different worlds. The important thing to remember is:

1. To understand the world(s) and then look for opportunities by identifying spaces in any relevant world that are not yet adequately filled (or to ask whether an already existing product is maximizing its presence within a given world).

2. To determine, once a product or brand is established in a world, if it is possible to expand its territorial claim within it.

3. To develop strategies to maintain its space against the encroachment of competitors. Share of World is different from Share of Market.

4. To explore possibilities for a product to play a role in another world.

Patagonia may stake out territory in the mid-level/periphery of the fashion world, but the more important territory it has staked out might be in the outdoor or environmentally conscious worlds, where it owns world share nearer to the core.

What we are proposing here is not something unknown, but our angle and our understanding of how it works is new, and we think it opens up new market-strategy possibilities that can build on the good work that is already being done by many forward-looking companies in their various markets. These companies are already pursuing the kind of branding strategies that we are proposing, but they are doing it without necessarily being aware of the larger process at work. What we propose to do here is to describe our current understanding about how cultural branding works as an element in a larger process we have already described regarding our world perspective model.

Our goal here is to detail five interconnected elements—social context, experience, community, products and services, and infrastructure sensibility—which synergistically combine to shape or structure activities within a given lifestyle world. These five components, which we represent as a series of concentric rings, encompass the range of salient "contact points" between a cultural brand and the consumers engaged in those activities. The inner three rings (social context, experience and community) have the most direct bearing on whether a brand develops into a "cultural" brand, but are also the most abstract and correspondingly difficult to manipulate. The outermost rings (products and services, and infrastructure sensibility) are conceptually more concrete than these other elements and represent what we traditionally consider the scope of "branding work." Although the hierarchy formed by these five rings might seem to suggest the innermost elements have a closer connection to the brand than the others, all five are equally important and must work in tandem to create a cultural brand. Put somewhat differently, one or the other of these five elements might be the thing that entices someone to enter a world in which the brand is prominent, but all five play a role in making him or her want to come back. Each element, as this atomic image suggests, functions as part of a larger structure that helps define a brand's cultural connection to the world.

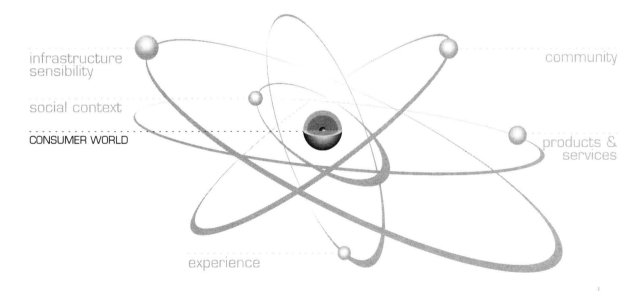

infrastructure sensibility

community

social context

CONSUMER WORLD

products & services

experience

element 1: social context

An important key to our understanding anything that is happening in the economic or political spheres of American, or any other, society requires understanding what is happening in the cultural sphere. This is the sphere in society traditionally shaped by educational and religious institutions, and now embraces the media and entertainment worlds. The cultural sphere of a society is where people derive their ideas about what makes their lives worth living; the economic sphere how they make a living; the political sphere how people with competing interests work out a way of living together. Activities in all three spheres actively shape any given society. But markets and politics tend to play a more reactive role than most people think.

Because most business people tend to operate within the economic and power spheres of society, we tend to discount the importance of the cultural sphere, which plays an equally dynamic role in shaping a society. Ideas matter. Values matter. And ideas and values develop and evolve within the cultural sphere. And for this reason it's important to recognize that the shift currently taking place within the cultural sphere in American society is having and will continue to have a significant shaping effect in the way we do business and the way we conduct our politics and our business.

the soul age

Much of what we have presented depends on understanding how the culture is adjusting from a set of values dominated by a masculine, rational/technological orientation to one that embraces a broader spectrum of values. It would be idiotic to suggest that rationality and technology will stop having a profound effect in shaping American and global society; we do think, however, that their influence is being recalibrated as it comes into a more balanced relationship with a broader range of concerns that we call "soul values."

However you conceptualize it, one thing is clear—since the 1960s what we have been calling soul values has been playing an increasingly influential role in shaping significant parts of American culture and lifestyle. We see it in the increasingly wider acceptance of alternative healthcare, in the amazing growth of organic food products, in the emergence of women's liberation movements, the continuing concern about environmental degradation, in the simplicity movement, and in so many other areas of American life, which are often radically opposed to the commercially/technologically oriented values that shaped mainstream culture throughout most of the last century. The concern about American society regaining its soul is a symptom of a deep cultural longing, and that is why the soul values-centered movements are not fads and why they are not going away. They reflect a deeper social psychological need and as such reflect a deeper kind of shift within American society's cultural sphere.

But it is also true to say that not everyone is attracted to or feels comfortable with soul values or wants to live a lifestyle completely circumscribed by them, but almost everyone knows someone whose lifestyle is influenced by them. It might be people at work or in the neighborhood, or it might even be one's spouse or kids. For some outside the world, there is no inclination to go in. For others, it is intriguing, and they might want to go in to find out what it's like inside.

The world of soul values is inhabited as much by extreme sports enthusiasts as it is with organic gardeners. It's as much the soul-patched Ohno as it is Deepak Chopra. Miles Davis as it is Enya.

retrieval: way forward is the way back

Before talking specifically about how soul values influence a particular lifestyle world, it might be useful to better understand a particular historical theme that is helpful for grasping what we mean by soul values. What we propose is much broader in scope than what, for instance, Paul Ray suggests in his discussion of "Cultural Creatives." One of the keys to understanding soul values is to understand their connection to traditional values whose origins lie in the pre-modern eras of Western and non-Western cultures. The cultural shift we are undergoing now can in part be understood as an attempt to retrieve and reintegrate elements from our pre-modern cultural heritage within the new kind of complex technologically driven society that has developed in the last 500 years.

This is a complex phenomenon and deserves more discussion than we can give it here, but the broad-strokes concept is this: If you want to understand the future, try to understand better what modern societies left behind. What the culture has lost to "modern progress," it wants now to retrieve, and that's the key to understanding what we mean by the soul age and soul values. Modern societies, dominated by commercial/technological values since the mid-19th Century, have become slick and soulless, and while hardly anyone complains about the material benefits that commercial/technological societies have generated, there is nevertheless a profound dissatisfaction with the fundamental soullessness that has become associated with them. There is a growing hunger now for anything that has a soulfulness about it.

What late moderns long for is what societies strongly influenced by pre-modern values still have. All healthy pre-modern cultures have a deep sense of connectedness to nature, to family and its elders, to tribe or community, and to the spiritual world; and many late moderns long for those things because they are missing in their lives. Traditional cultures produce things by hand, not machines. The art is beautiful but not slick; simple and accessible, not esoteric and impossible to understand. Time is not measured by clocks. Space is not something where things are experienced as separated from one another but rather as interrelated as in a medieval tapestry.

"Connection" is the characteristic experience for the pre-modern; "disconnection," fragmentation and alien-

HARTBEAT 2.2 the coming fusion culture

Assimilation is what used to happen to immigrants when we thought that America was a big melting pot. Immigrants arrived as young men and women, adapting as necessity required to their new environment, but still living very much out of the traditions and values of their culture of origin. And as they grew older they watched as their children became more American, and as their grandchildren grew up with hardly any sense at all of the kind of world from which their grandparents came.

The grandkids, maybe when they're older, will take an interest in their ethnic heritage, but it will have been too late. It will be a kind of hobby, not something that they live from as their grandparents did. We create museums for those elements in our culture that are no longer alive, and for the third and fourth generations and beyond the traditions of their grandparents have become, for the most part, museum pieces. These later generations have become Americans.

It's a different story, though, for the Caribbean and Asian people who have come to this country since the 1970s because, for all kinds of reasons, there just isn't the same kind of Anglo-dominated mainstream culture for them to assimilate into anymore. What it means to be an American has been rapidly changing in the last 30 years. The old Anglo culture is still there, of course, and for now it's still very influential in the government and corporate halls of power, but we are seeing more and more people, mostly kids, who are prodigiously adaptive to any number of cultural influences, and they move from one subculture into another with equally prodigious ease. That's what the sociologists mean by "multi-acculturation."

But we doubt this will remain a permanent feature in American society. In a few generations' time we will be seeing the emergence of a global fusion culture mediated through the inevitably homogenizing power of electronic information technologies. This fusion culture will draw from the pre-modern traditions of Asian, African, Latin American and various indigenous cultures, but in an increasingly hi-tech idiom.

This fusion will occur most easily in the U.S. where there is already hardly any vestige of the pre-modern world, but will slowly transform even those societies in Asia or the Middle East or Africa or Latin America where pre-modern cultural forms are still strong. It's not just about what happens to people who immigrate here; it's about the cultures that they import with them that are being slowly woven into the fusion culture and how that will be exported back to the cultures from which they came. This trend will be abetted by what we're exporting through the Internet and MTV. Rap, for instance, started in inner-city black culture and is now a style imitated throughout the world. A global style is something you can see already everywhere, and this is just the beginning.

All traditional ethnic identity is rooted in pre-modern cultural forms, and the pre-modern roots of cultural identity will all but disappear by the end of this century. They won't go without a fight, as we're seeing now in the Islamic world, but we're convinced that ethnicity or any rigidly defined traditionalist worldview is simply fading as a dominating source of cultural identity. Ethnic identities simply will not be able to withstand the enormous consciousness-changing and power of the new information technologies.

There will be from time to time moments of nostalgia when it will be cool to get into one's ethnicity and to search for one's "roots." And there will continue to be enclaves of traditionalists who reject the postmodern fusion culture. But they'll just live like the Amish live in Pennsylvania or the Hasids in Brooklyn. They'll just keep to themselves and vote, if they vote at all, for whoever promises to leave them alone.

But the future does not lie in that kind of nostalgic clinging to the past. This is different from saying that the past isn't important for the future. The past will have an enormously important influence on the way we shape lifestyles in the fusion culture. That's where "retrieval" comes in. Retrieval is not about going back to the way things were, but of salvaging the all-but-lost elements—valued for their soulfulness—from fading pre-modern cultural traditions. The goal of retrieval is to integrate cultural elements from the past into a postmodern lifestyle that gives it more "soul," and this will be done in an eclectic, irrational way that will be very hard to predict except for its general outlines.

What exactly that means and how that plays out is the burning question. People will take what's soulful wherever they find it, whether it's from Asian spiritualities or African music and graphic arts, Shaker furniture or Mediterranean cuisine. The new Soul Culture will be a Fusion Culture driven by a longing to retrieve what's soulful from pre-modern cultural traditions integrated with and mediated by a postmodern information tech style.

Multi-acculturation leads to inevitable fusion. And understanding the social dynamics that are driving American (and eventually global) society toward fusion is at the heart of what we mean by understanding "trends" in the Soul Age.

by Jack Whelan

ation are more characteristic of the late modern experience. The emphasis on individuals and their rights to do as they please with little regard for the common good is a central element of modernity. And this in turn has led to the social fragmentation in which hardly any social bond is valued more highly than one's individuality and freedom.

Immigrants or visitors to America who come from cultures where the old traditional, communal values still have some influence are shocked when they discover how the elderly are treated here—and at the crime, alienation, violence and loneliness that they find as well. In commercial/technological societies there is comparatively little sense of belonging to a larger group. Moderns are on their own in a way that would be inconceivable in a traditional culture. So connection, warmth, immediacy, humor, authenticity, intensity are all elements that shape the world of soul values, and they are what late modern Americans find missing and long to retrieve.

We believe that much of the thrust into the Soul Age is driven by a longing to recover this lost sense of soulful connection. And it's the charm of their lingering pre-modern traditions that makes, for instance, a visit to "tradition-centered" cultures in Europe, Asia or Africa interesting to Americans for whom such traditions never really existed, except for a few years among its newly arrived immigrants and their children. But ethnic traditions, while they might stay alive in pockets here and there, eventually shrivel as third and fourth generations assimilate into the commercial/technological/media-centered culture that has played the principal role in shaping American society during the 20th Century. Even though a tradition-centered lifestyle is one few moderns would want to live themselves, many moderns want these traditional cultures preserved so they can take interesting travel vacations to places where they can experience their soulful charm.

Now how does all this relate to markets for products and services? If the culture is shifting, the markets have to adapt. And if we're right about the shift to soul values, then the marketers have to adjust to the changing needs and values of an increasing number of consumers who are looking for products, services, experiences and communications that reflect their need for a more soulfulness in their lives. Our world model is a useful tool because it can help marketers to predict where things are going within the larger culture, but also within any of a number of niche cultures that compose contemporary American society. If marketers keep their eyes on what is interesting to the trendsetters in the core of any given world, they will be given significant clues about what will become more widely accepted in the future, even if for now it interests only an esoteric few.

So while that's true for any specific lifestyle world, we are also saying that all these worlds are caught up in a larger movement in which commercial/technological values are becoming increasingly balanced by soul values. So the people who are the innovators at the core of these new soul-centered lifestyle worlds are bellweathers for the rest of the culture.

element 2: experience

A soul-oriented culture world is different from a rational culture world in that it is subjective-experience oriented rather than objective-truth oriented. Value within the rational paradigm is linked to abstract and cerebral functioning. Value in the soul paradigm is linked to intensity of experience—it's visceral, gritty, emotional. It is precisely because so many Americans find that so much of their life is hyper-organized and technologized that they long for the non-rational dimensions of experience valued in soul-oriented cultures. They are looking for balance, and that balance is presented to them by the emergence of various soul-oriented lifestyle worlds. And one of the ways to find your soul is by having intense experiences, and the possibility for having such experiences is often linked to a retrieval of the experiences of the more primitive, pre-technological past.

At the end of the work week, some of us might wander out into the woods, content to explore nature the way our ancestors did. But more and more Americans contract the services of a mountaineering guide, invest a lot of time and money in intricate outdoor gear, and travel into nature to engage in an "authentic wilderness experience." Similarly, whereas cattle drives, fruit harvests and archeological digs were once considered sheer drudgery—grunt work delegated to the low-skilled among us—consumers are now willing to pay top dollar for the chance to engage in these carefully managed, "authentic" experiences. In a world where successes and failures are measured by the tiny bits of electronic information composing a bank balance, we crave the chance to experience for ourselves the gritty realities that confronted our more soulful ancestors.

This experience orientation isn't limited to recreating the past. Themed, experiential retail environments— staged for the enactment of authentic experiences—are populating the retail landscape. While most of us have some familiarity with the early precursors—Niketown, Planet Hollywood and Hard Rock Café—perhaps the best illustration of this idea put into practice is REI's flagship store in Seattle. Opened in September 1996, the store's featured attractions include the world's tallest indoor climbing structure; an outdoor, mountain-bike test trail; a boot-test trail with "non-trivial" steepness; water filter testing stations; and an indoor rain room (for testing water-resistant gear under inclement conditions). Under one roof, the "outdoor" consumer can now engage in an array of carefully managed "authentic" experiences. It is no longer enough to merely sell stuff, forward-thinking retailers must also create, manage and sell experience.

While most people in business have an intuitive sense that this craving for experience is starting to matter, the topic remains largely unaddressed in the business literature. An important exception is Pine and Gilmore's 1999 work, *The Experience Economy*, in which the authors distinguish experiences from services. In doing so, they set experience up to be the next evolutionary phase of the world economy, following in the footsteps of its predecessors—the agrarian, industrial and service economies. As they contend, "From now on, leading-edge companies—whether they sell to consumers or businesses—will find that the next competitive battleground lies in staging experiences."

Their work neatly dovetails what our research has uncovered with regard to lifestyle marketing, which has yielded important insights about the nature and influence of experience. We will first describe what we consider to be the key dimensions of experience (emotion and utility) and will then describe five elements of experience (knowledge, community, authenticity, relevance and surprise).

emotion vs. utility

Emotional factors are those that are visceral, engage the senses and spark an affective reaction. They include feeling part of a community, trusting store personnel and participating in a shopping *experience*. They impart a sense that the store smells like it should, the personnel are knowledgeable and helpful, and the management cares about its customers. Additionally, whether people shop for emotional reasons often depends on the product category for which they are shopping. The experience of shopping at REI's flagship store—while taking in the sights and sounds of this wonderfully staged shopping event—is a good example of this emotional appeal and how it can be used by retailers. Driving a Harley-Davidson is another example of something that is emotional and "gritty." This—along with the identity traits attached to the bike, the values of the company and the community that surround the use of the product—is the appeal of a Harley.

Utility factors, on the other hand, take into account day-to-day routines. Utility factors include such ideas as convenience and habit. Consumers who shop for products for utility reasons are often short on time, do not care about non-utility related differences between stores, products and brands (such as authenticity, knowledgeable salespeople, experience, etc.) and are often less involved with product details. Most consumers shop for at least some products for utility. In the wellness lifestyle world, for example, consumers at different levels of wellness involvement shop for wellness products differently. Core wellness consumers value many of the emotional aspects that go along with shopping for wellness products, while periphery consumers are influenced more by utility factors. Additionally, different channels are associated with different emotion and utility characteristics.

With these factors in mind, we can now turn to the elements of experience.

1. community—Tucked beneath the shadow of globalization's looming front, cultural analysts and historians have been busy documenting the surprising (to some) resurgence of interest in localized community for quite a spell now. While there has been much interest in evolving notions of community with regard to developments in the communications infrastructure (e.g., the now tired notion that the Internet could allow for the possibility of communities not bound

HARTBEAT 2.3 sometimes an experience is just an experience

We aren't the first to point out the importance of the retail shopping experience to marketers, but there's something fascinating about how this experience has affected shopping in modern America that even we have failed to mention. You can witness this new behavior at any of the more successful experience retailers. For example, on a recent expedition through our local natural foods store, an employee in the produce department casually explained that the crowd of shoppers making it nearly impossible to move was not actually there to buy ("No thanks, just looking"). I was surprised, not at his observation, but at the nonchalance with which he volunteered it. Was this just employee apathy? No, far from indifference his reply conveyed a sense of accommodation. You see he'd seen it all before.

The shopper as tourist phenomenon is no longer confined to regionally progressive enclaves either. In Kroger's Cincinnati backyard is a grocery store called Jungle Jim's, "Where grocery shopping is always an ADVENTURE," according to their web site. Don't believe what you read? Reserve a spot on their one-hour store walking tour and see for yourself. What I find amusing, aside from the Jungle's life-sized mechanical bears belting out The King's, "You Ain't Nothin' But a Hound Dog," is Kroger's response to the local consumers' overwhelming endorsement of this Cincinnati upstart. Whereas Jungle constructed thematically interesting ethnic quarters to display a mix of familiar and exotic foods from around the world, Kroger's spin was to plant a miniature Italian flag next to the spaghetti sauce shelf, a little Union Jack next to the marmalade, etc. You won't find curious shoppers scrutinizing the Kroger display of dill pickles any time soon. At least not in the same way they go foraging for exotic Indian pickles and chutney at Jungle Jim's. Still, to its credit, Kroger knows it has to play the retail experience game.

Every retailer should play the game in order to stem the exodus of their customers to the stores that get it, but, and this finally is my point, even retailers who successfully market the wellness experience risk losing customers. Providing an experience is all well and good, consumers clearly love it, but at the end of the day stores still need sales. Consumers who just look, who just experience without buying anything, represent lost sales as much as consumers who never stop in. Experience retailers definitely have the foot traffic, but too many of their shoppers continue to spend their cash elsewhere.

To add injury to insult, we know that many of the consumers who fail to buy certain products while shopping in particular stores go on to purchase those very products elsewhere. I'm not merely describing the ubiquitous multi-channel shopper. I'm talking about someone who goes to the grocery store every week to buy food and sundries, yet still finds it necessary to check out from the grocery store, load up their car, negotiate traffic and fight for another parking spot at some other store, only to buy something they could have found at the grocery store they just left. Is this a rare phenomenon, isolated to the peculiar habits of (hard) core consumers? Hardly, our research shows this pattern of shopping behavior is now widespread, affecting every major channel for every major product category.

Has homo economicus suddenly turned insensatus? Probably not. I suspect it really has something to do with retail tourism, but I can only guess at why. My suspicion is that retailers have only partly nailed down the experience. Shoppers still carry expectations about what products particular channels should carry or, more importantly, what products they will purchase. If, for example, the experience encountered in a particular grocery store does not create the feeling that, say, organics belong, then consumers will not buy organics from that store. They'll go elsewhere until the grocery store experience fosters the expectation that it's okay to buy organics at the regular grocery store.

Not only does the experience have to be relevant to the shopper, it has to relate to the products as well. A wonderful experience can easily wind up as a terrific attraction, rather than a reason to buy. Does this mean retailers now have to be all things to all consumers? Only if they want to sell everything to everybody. In the meantime, it means expect to see consumers just tour stores as retailers develop and refine the experiences that encourage buying as much as shopping.

By David Moore, Ph.D.

by space—virtual communities), we find that most folks still think about community the good old-fashioned way. Briefly, communities are groups of people with a common bond that develop in or around "the local areas where people live and do stuff."

Central to the notion of experience is human interaction, which includes other shoppers as well as store personnel. The shopping experience is inherently social, and the interaction, whether positive or negative, directly and indirectly affects purchase decisions. Beyond inter-action, community operates on many levels. There is the immediate community context created by the store environment. There is the diffuse abstract community of consumers formed by virtue of shared interests and values. There is the virtual community that the store represents through symbols, gestures, design, etc. And, of course, there is the local community in which the store operates. All of these interlocking levels of community raise emotion by providing a sense of belonging—that one is at home with friends and family.

2. knowledge—Knowledge constitutes a significant portion of the potential value added by retailers and manufacturers. We know that consumers at the core of any lifestyle world crave knowledge about the products they buy, so having knowledgeable store personnel and other

organizing principles of experience that drive emotion

principle	mechanism	emotion
community	interaction	belonging
knowledge	empowerment	confidence
authenticity	trust	security
relevance	personal connection	comfort
surprise	delight	pleasure

means to communicate useful information is a significant part of the shopping experience. Knowledge, in the sense of information transfer, takes several different forms. It can be information about the store, about products or about events and activities pertinent to consumers. Regardless of what the subject matter is, the key is to be the purveyor of information providing consumers the space and opportunity to pick and choose what fits their lifestyle. Indeed, knowledge can contribute powerfully to a consumer's sense of community. Fundamentally, knowledge empowers consumers to act in an informed way, which can raise a retailer's emotional appeal by increasing consumer confidence.

While predicting emerging trends is never an infallible exercise, we can offer a few insights to emerging experience-based trends in the retail sector. First, expect to find an engaging dialogue at all levels of the retail experience. Here, the goal is to engage the customer in a dialogue regarding some aspect of a highly differentiated product or service category. It will no longer be enough to simply place supplements, for example, on a shelf and expect them to sell well. Instead, customers will be responding to thoughtful education and recommendations from trained experts and knowledgeable professionals.

We should add here that the phrase "trained experts and knowledgeable professionals" means just that. We are not talking about well-intentioned, interested employees. We're suggesting certified nutritionists, pharmacists, etc. with concise authoritative information. Similarly, wine should no longer be sold with shelf tags or recommendations from the produce department. Instead, a trained sommelier will provide that service.

3. authenticity—Authenticity, like knowledge, is a consumption dimension, but it is much more complex as part of experience. Depending on what kind of experience one wants, being the real deal can make shopping part of a lifestyle rather than simply the means for procuring goods. On the other hand, the authenticity of an extreme experience may raise as much con-

It hit me the other day that authenticity is a Catch-22. The big companies that have the resources to communicate authenticity rarely have it, and the small companies that have it don't have the resources to communicate it. Authenticity is intrinsically elusive, hard to create and, like seafood, is only good when it's fresh.

Small entrepreneurial companies are naturally authentic because the owner/founder/key manager is their brand. They live it, breathe it and are passionately committed to it. And it shows, in all their messy, sometimes confusing, but always authentic meanderings. But big company managers charged with branding are professionals. And the trouble is that the subvocal message that shoppers pick up is: "These guys were selling fast food burgers yesterday, and today they're trying to sell me a wellness product? Give me a break." So what's a big brand manager to do? We think the answer is not in what you say but who you are. That is, who you really are.

You may or may not remember the Merry Pranksters, Ken Keasey's band of crazed hippies who crossed America in a painted bus with a destination plate that read "FURTHER." Just reading Tom Wolfe's recounting of the Merry Pranksters adventures in The Electric Kool-Aid Acid Test should be sufficient to break the most buttoned-up of MBAs into a sweat of authenticity. Even though few people ever actually saw them and even fewer ever "got on the bus," the Merry Pranksters' trip across America was a catalyzing event and catapulted them to a long-term place in America's Zeitgeist. The answer for them was in the abandon of their old lives, paying attention to the real, the now and what moved them. The answer for you will be the same.

So who does authenticity well? One of the best examples I can think of is Odwalla juices from Half Moon Bay, CA. You discover Odwalla by the free-standing refrigerated case in grocery stores and the like. The bright colors and wild designs harken to a rainforest. Their pledge "juice for humans" is about as far from packaged-goods adspeak as it comes. And, as soon as you see the products, you immediately understand that these people are the genuine thing. They're obviously comfortable with themselves and what they do. Antioxidants aren't some exotic chemical that an R&D technologist has suggested adding to their products. It's an inherent property of the mangoes and cranberries. The echinacea in their cold fighter is a natural outgrowth of their lifestyle, not a fad nutraceutical. Heck. They even make spirulina and wheatgrass taste good. But what's most important is the sum of the parts. When you stand back from their cooler and ask yourself what's being communicated here you stop seeing products and start seeing a window. The sum total of their communication is a window into a better, "more well" lifestyle. And the invitation says: "Pick me up and try me, I can help you feel terrific." It's compelling, believable, and it works.

By Harvey Hartman

cern as excitement and effectively scare off consumers. Like the participants in the cattle drive depicted in *City Slickers*, we want it real, just not too real. In these instances, consumer research can pinpoint potential problems and reveal the essential elements necessary to convey authenticity without fear. Authenticity conveys information, insofar as the term "authentic" connotes high efficacy, good quality, shared values, etc. More importantly, however, authenticity instills trust.

Starbucks didn't create a global coffee empire by paying a lot of attention to the production and distribution of coffee and related products. Nor did Starbucks engage in massive, high-concept advertising campaigns. Instead, Starbucks focused on creating and managing the coffee experience, one store at a time. Their retail "coffee shops" are living, breathing shrines to the authentic coffee experience. Step on up to the counter and watch as a "trained barista" (no mere employee) builds the perfect coffee drink before your very eyes. The authentic aromas of recently roasted coffee abound. Next, proceed to the lounge where one can relax next to a fireplace and converse with friends from the neighborhood. In short, going to Starbucks is an experience.

4. relevance—Because an individualized lifestyle in part fulfills consumers' desires for a size that does not fit all, having an experience that feels personalized carries greater weight than one that caters to some common denominator. To make an experience connect on a personal level, in turn, presupposes that it somehow relates to consumers' lifestyles. For example, we have found that any experience relevant to consumers will allow them to participate on their own terms, in effect, creating their own brand.

As an example, our current research indicates that many consumers have tired of governmental and scientific pronouncements on what constitutes a healthy diet. In reaction to these dietary strictures and other constraints, consumers now seek choices that permit them to participate in wellness at a level they find comfortable. Thus, experiences that increase consumer comfort by allowing them to express their individuality and by fitting into their lifestyles will appeal more positively than will experiences that essentially dictate the terms.

Another example, Starbucks creates each drink customized to the individual consumer. It is not unusual for Starbucks consumers to make requests for sometimes elaborate drinks designed just for them.

5. surprise—For many, part of the attraction of shopping is the act of discovery. What makes shopping in a Mediterranean bazaar exciting is not knowing what you will find. Even if your

intent is to find a nice sweater to bring home as a gift, the shopping experience is enhanced tenfold by the possibility of finding something that you were not looking for. If an experience can raise a mundane shopping trip to the level of an adventure, the consumer is apt to want to repeat the experience. Surprise, as a component of the shopping experience, is not synonymous with change. In fact, due to consumer expectations, change can often provoke negative reactions by confusing and frustrating consumers accustomed to a particular routine.

Surprise does not mean, for instance, changing the store organization every few weeks. People like to know where they have to go to find the eggs or the cucumbers or the ice cream. Surprise means finding something different alongside other things that they expect to find there. Surprise means keeping things fresh. It's about adding to the experience, not subtracting from it. Indeed, some stores incorporate surprise, in the form of fresh new products and suggestions, as part of their routine so that shoppers plan return visits expressly to delight in the latest addition. Being pleasantly surprised heightens the emotional appeal of the shopping experience and brings customers back in search of the next surprise.

The best kind of shopping experience is one that raises emotion as well as utility, and the hot-buttons for this kind of experience spring from the primary organizing principles of experience: community, knowledge, authenticity, relevance and surprise. While much of our analysis of experience has been confined to the importance of experience in retail outlets, much of what has been described above can also be applied by the manufacturer to capitalize on what Pine and Gilmore have pointed to as the economy of the new millennium. In short, we can create experience brands.

Finally, we would like to make one last observation. If Pine and Gilmore's assertions are correct that experience represents the next evolutionary phase of the world economy, then it stands to reason that those who control access to authentic experiences will be best positioned to command brand equity and price premiums. In such a world, economic power and profits won't likely emanate from economies of scale, production efficiencies or manufacturing concerns. Instead, retailers, merchandisers and designers will likely be driving the successful branding campaigns—and revenue streams—of the experience economy. Among other things, this suggests that manufacturers lacking the means or power to shape and control experience may increasingly find themselves delegated to the production of private label brands for third parties.

The genius of Starbucks was its vision to build thousands of stages on which the theater of coffee experience is played out daily. Following in this vision, Starbucks only recently began offering their signature coffees in retail grocers. Only now, once most customers have had some exposure to the "authentic" coffee experience, has Starbucks even bothered with the mainstream retail grocery arena. If Pine and Gilmore are correct, we imagine there will be plenty of displaced manufacturers vying for the contract-production business of the visionaries with the foresight to enter the experience economy.

element 3: community

People like the freedom that comes with living in a fragmented culture where nobody knows or much cares what you do with your private life. But they also feel disconnected, isolated and cut off; and that part of it they don't much like. People want to have the freedom to enter a world on their own terms, but they also want to participate in something that is bigger than themselves. People want to feel a part of something. This is, for instance, the appeal of being a sports fan and going to the game. Watching the game in the stadium is a completely different experience from watching it at home alone on TV. What makes it different is the visceral experience of being part of this larger social organism called "the crowd."

That's a part of what it means to be in a community—to have the visceral experience of connecting to a larger social reality. And stepping into the world of a particular sports team is stepping into a world that has all the essential elements of what we call a "brand community," and it comprises a core, mid-level and periphery like all the worlds we've described so far. You don't have to be a hard-core fan to experience the world, but to the degree that you only participate on the periphery, you don't really come to feel like a member of the community.

Instead a peripheral fan when entering a brand community should at the very least recognize that there is a community. He may or may not be attracted to it. But if he is attracted, he will probably (gradually) move from the periphery of the world toward the core. And any deeper involvement in that world will require becoming part of its community, and therefore one of the marks that distinguishes a peripheral participant in a world from those who participate in the mid-level or core is the degree to which he feels a part of lifestyle or brand culture's community. In a sports-fan brand world, those kinds of community experiences might involve developing a relationship with nearby season ticket holders or finding a sports bar "where everybody knows your name." In either case, the individual finds others with whom he identifies to share his experience within a brand community.

But while many people like having places where they can go where they are anonymous and can be left alone, they also don't like being there for too long. Most people need to have some social connection where they feel they belong, where people *do* know their name, and this is not a experience taken for granted in the kind of fragmented social environment many Americans experience today, particularly those in America's cities and suburbs.

Identity, one's sense of self, one's sense of being a "somebody," depends to a large extent on how that is

Understanding that language and cultural values are deeply intertwined, and ultimately define who we are and how we relate to each other, is the basis of our analysis of conversations with consumers. Although our research is conducted in the United States, primarily among English-speaking consumers, not every speaker of the English language will talk the same way. Rather, there are individual and social variations that make it possible to segment and typify consumers through a linguistic filter. The language consumers use to describe personal attitudes about relationships, typically expressed as abstract ideals, reveals general value systems about community (networks of personal relationships). The word list to the right, not ranked in any particular order, illustrates language that is commonly used to describe these values.

Relationship Values

Honest
Trustworthy
Having Integrity
Loving/Caring
Humorous
Intelligent
Attractive
Creative
Hard Working
Flexible

Why is it important to analyze language and uncover relationship values among consumers? Simply put, the meanings consumers apply to personal relationships can be translated to meanings consumers apply to choosing a brand. In other words, when choosing a brand, many consumers talk about the importance of an "honest" brand, a company with "integrity," or advertising campaigns that are "intelligent" and "creative." These socially shared meanings (use of language) and practices link consumers, making them feel as if they are part of an extended relationship or community.

Benefits of Relationships

Safety
Security
Familiarity
Balance
Delight
Excitement
Knowledge
Sustainability
Intimacy
Empowerment

The importance of understanding community values is not only useful in achieving meaningful communication with consumers, but in realizing the latent benefits consumers derive. As we talk with consumers about their life desires, goals, frustrations and fears, we find that the benefits they hope to gain through relationships fulfills certain needs, which in turn, motivates behavior. Consumers' perceptions of community benefits, not ranked in order, is illustrated to the right:

Variation in consumers' responses to relationship values and benefits allows us to profile and segment consumers into discrete shopper subgroups. For example, two consumers may hierarchically organize these benefits in different ways:

Consumer A	Consumer B
Safety	Balance
Security	Knowledge
Familiarity	Empowerment
Knowledge	Sustainability
Empowerment	Intimacy
Excitement	Safety
Delight	Delight
Intimacy	Excitement
Balance	Security
Sustainability	Familiarity

Variation in use and the ranking of these values or benefits don't necessarily mean that one order is more or less "simple" or that another is more or less "evolved." The differences are more complicated than that; they serve as expressions of alternative realities or other possible ways of thinking about things. These different ways of thinking indicate different ways of shopping. In other words, if a consumer is motivated by the benefits of security and familiarity, we are likely to find that they are traditional shoppers who are unlikely to experiment with products, may be very brand loyal, and are driven by dimensions of price and product efficacy. In contrast, a consumer motivated by the benefits of knowledge and sustainability are likely to be information gatherers, move quickly from product to product, and may be seeking brands that represent social sustainability such as locally grown products and brands.

Overall, linguistic differences indicate a cultural shift that is moving towards a new way of thinking about community and how it transfers to the marketplace. We are able to explore language use in every conceivable category, whether apples, soda or recycled paper towels. These sub-worlds cannot be separated from the language used to talk about them.

Qualitative language analysis illuminates the notion that language and culture are inextricably linked, that they are connected and evolve simultaneously. Through consideration of basic words that resonate with the consumer, depending on the social context and where they are situated in a given world of activity, manufacturers and retailers can not only interpret how consumers relate to one another but also identify spaces where connections can be made with consumers that extend beyond product or the physical retail environment. What better way to communicate with consumers than by speaking their language.

by Michelle Barry, Ph.D.

reflected back to him by those around him. And in order for someone to say with confidence that she is "this kind of person," she needs others to affirm that she is who she thinks she is, and that means being able to go somewhere where there are people who are capable of recognizing who she is. It takes one to know one. This can be done negatively, as for instance when a Mariner's fan goes to Yankee Stadium all decked out in Mariner regalia with the intent of inviting hometown abuse. Or a gun-control zealot going to a National Rifle Association convention to pass out gun control literature. This is one way that a person can affirm his identity and the depth of his values and convictions.

The more typical course of action would be to look for positive affirmations in joining with those whose values you share. Even the zealots need to go back to their community if for no other reason to allay fears that they might be crazy. "I am this kind of person with these specific values, and I'm not crazy, because look at all these others who share that sense of what's important. I belong here. These are my people. I feel accepted and understood here."

So the values of a particular community might differ radically from the values of the groups a person may be affiliated with, and yet it doesn't take long for anyone who enters a different world to catch on to how things are different. The traditions and rituals and language of groups are the key markers that celebrate those differences. For instance a visitor to Chicago might decide to take in a Cubs game at Wrigley Field, one America's great shrines to baseball tradition, and a place with many of its own rituals that define it as a

HARTBEAT 2.6 professional sports: soul culture or business culture?

Most fans when they go to the game to root for their local team go with a pre-modern, soul-centered mentality. They expect their players to behave like tribal warriors exhibiting the soul virtues of courage, loyalty to teammates, love of the home city.

But hardly anybody is Cal Ripken these days. Most players see themselves as modern businessmen where none of these values plays a significant role in their decision making. If anything, they would be considered foolish by the other players and management to let those values get in the way of a higher paycheck somewhere else. That's how things work within the player lifestyle world, a world structured very differently from the fan lifestyle world.

So it's understandable that fans boo when Alex Rodriguez comes back to Seattle as a Texas Ranger. But it also explains why his teammates don't see him as a traitor. It's a business, and his big paycheck today means a bigger one for them tomorrow.

The fans, however, do see him as having betrayed them. The players just think the fans are irrational because they don't understand how player culture operates. And the fans are irrational—or at least inconsistent. Because the same fans, when asked if they were offered the $250 million offered to A-Rod, say that they would have taken it, too.

The fans are caught between two worlds. One soulless and mercenary and the other where they expect their players to feel the same soulful connection to the fans that the fans feel for their champions.

By Jack Whelan

particular community within that larger tradition.

Such a visitor to Wrigley, might be shocked to have one of the people sitting near him come back from the beer stand and just give him a beer even though he didn't ask for it or pay for it. Among the many traditions at Wrigley, in certain sections of the stadium, is the expectation that if anyone goes to get a beer for himself, he brings back a few for the people sitting around him whether they asked for it or not, whether he knows them or not. This is a great community-building ritual because it conveys to someone who might be only

characteristics of a brand community

CHARACTERISTIC	DEFINITION	COMMUNITY BEHAVIOR	MANAGEMENT STRATEGY
Identity Enhancement	Individual enlarges sense of Self by participating in a community	I'm a Cubs fan, and I'm proud of it. I belong here.	Foster informal ways for customers to interact and to create "brand chemistry."
Rituals & Traditions	Individual feels a part of a proud tradition, which is celebrated by community rituals	When you buy a beer for yourself, you buy one for those around you.	It's important that rituals have authentic quality and not feel contrived. Equally important not to dilute meaning of existing rituals. First pitch becoming increasingly meaningless. Some rituals can be performed by employees who invite customers to participate.
Social Markers	People need some visible way of identifying themselves as community members and sometimes to indicate what their rank is within the community.	Team hats and Jerseys. Car decals, antenna ornaments and bumper stickers. Owning season tickets. Face and body painting.	The sales opportunities are obvious.
Moral Responsibility	Individuals affirm their membership in the group by behaving in a way that honors group codes, traditions, and rituals.	Standing and singing The Star-Spangled Banner with hats off; Seventh Inning Stretch; buy neighbors a beer when it's your turn.	Moral standards are best policed by the customers themselves (usually by their shaming offenders into compliance), but employees should intervene when necessary.
Bottom–Up Dynamic	Customers play a significant role in shaping product design, innovations and experience	Rally Monkey at Angels games. Drummers at Oakland A's games.	Management needs to be particularly attentive to innovations intitiated by the customers themselves, and to do its best to nurture such organic initiatives where appropriate or just get out of the way.

the most peripheral of participants that this is the way things are done around here, and you can belong, too, if you follow the rules. It's a ritual that breaks down the walls of anonymity that are more typical these days among strangers, and conveys a sense of trust that the people will honor the tradition. It relies on a sense of trust that if I take care of those around me, they'll take care of me. People want to come back to such a world, and they enjoy participating in those kinds of rituals. They have soul.

Other major league teams might learn from this. The Cubs teams don't win, but the fans come anyway. Being a Cub fan means more to them than just winning. And the same logic applies to almost any business. Customers will come back, even if they have to pay premium prices, if there is something "more" for them that draws them back. One of these factors is the sense of belonging to a community.

element 4: products & services

Within the context of cultural branding, there are two main types of products. The first embraces those products which in and of themselves generate a brand culture, the best known examples being products like Harley-Davidson motorcycles, Apple Computers, The Grateful Dead, certain (not all) sports franchises, as in our Chicago Cubs example. There are other opportunities here, but these products and brands are relatively rare, and they are often the product of good luck as much as they are savvy strategic marketing. But they are interesting to study because of the way in which they create a world that can be analyzed using the tools we have laid out above.

The second category embraces those far more numerous products that need an existing lifestyle world in which to play a role. The mainstream brands established in the '50s and '60s by the great mainstream consumer products companies like Proctor & Gamble, General Mills and General Electric or retailers like Sears and Safeway functioned effectively in a more homogenous American culture whose lifestyle was easier to understand and whose purchasing behavior was easier to predict. The understanding about how products and brands functioned to support the mainstream American lifestyle during that era is compatible with what we want to say now about the greater variety of lifestyle worlds in a fragmented marketplace.

People still need toothpaste and ice cream, but the success of Tom's of Maine toothpaste and Ben & Jerry's ice cream are indicators of how commodity products that don't have an established foothold in the American cultural psyche need to position themselves. And they send a cautionary message to those who have well-established products and brands, because their market share will gradually diminish as people come gradually to ally themselves with the growing number of niche lifestyle markets and the products that better support them. A lot of people today buy Crest toothpaste. Even more would buy it if there were no Tom's on the scene. Market share is gradually becoming less relevant as a measure of marketing effectiveness,

HARTBEAT 2.7 the grateful dead: a classic cultural brand

We direct attention toward one last example in which a pronounced emphasis on community resulted in substantial profits, long-term financial stability and an almost unrivaled degree of brand loyalty: The Grateful Dead.

From their very incarnation, the Grateful Dead were as involved with building a community as they were with their music. And at every turn—conscious or unconscious—their business decisions magically reflected this interest. Sure, the business stuff was important, but the Grateful Dead also realized that without their community, there might not be a "business side." Early on, for example, the band decided that it was important, wherever possible, to hire their own private security firms to oversee security operations at the band's concerts; a move necessitated, in large part, by the significant amount of open drug use at these concerts. By hiring private security firms, the band could essentially direct security to "look the other way" at activities that other security personnel might pursue with legal intervention. While many saw this decision as irrational from a business standpoint (why should the band have to incur the added expense?), the Grateful Dead quite correctly realized that it isn't very easy for one's fan base to purchase recordings from a jail cell. (The legality of this, of course, is not the issue.)

Similarly, their now infamous decision to let audience members at their concerts make audio recordings for personal use—a decision that defied all rational business logic at the time—now appears a stroke of pure genius. You see, most conventional recording artists of the day, concerned with royalties and licensing revenues, would never have allowed audience members and fans to make audio recordings of live performances. After all, the argument went, if fans were allowed to make recordings for personal use, why would they then purchase commercial recordings? As the Grateful Dead found out, perhaps unwittingly, one of the unintended by-products of allowing fans to make audio recordings was that the world of activity centered around the Grateful Dead grew much larger and more cohesive. Entire networks of relationships developed as thousands of fans, spread across many continents, swapped stories and traded tapes. In essence, the community was strengthened and enlarged through an innovative—yet nonetheless genuine—route to active participation.

In the end, this push toward community proved quite profitable. As John Perry Barlow, lyricist for the Grateful Dead is fond of pointing out:

> We have been letting people tape our concerts since the early '70s, but instead of reducing the demand for our product, we are now the largest concert draw in America, a fact that is at least in part attributable to the popularity generated by those tapes.

Though perhaps arrived at accidentally, this, we submit, was a very forward-thinking business strategy.

speaking of brand loyalty...

Of course we've yet to address the most compelling case for the power of community. That is, how did the Grateful Dead convince a significant number of people from diverse—and at times "questionable"—socioeconomic backgrounds to leave their jobs, follow the band around the globe, and be content to spend most of their remaining money on concert tickets and related accoutrements? The answer certainly doesn't lie in the Grateful Dead's amazing musicianship or songwriting ability (they were never widely regarded for either). Nor, for that matter, does the answer lie in the band's unrivalled popularity (to this day, they are rarely heard on the radio). No, the answer is to be found in the power of community. The genius of the Grateful Dead was to be content providing the stage and scenery within which authentic, indigenous community action took place. Once that feat was accomplished, the question of whether or not to attend a Grateful Dead concert or purchase a recording was really moot—one did these things simply because one was a member of the extended clan.

The Grateful Dead never followed a branding textbook because they never needed to, it just came naturally to them. Perhaps someday soon a generation of branding students will glance up long enough to realize that the future of marketing and retailing lies not in clever advertising campaigns or quirky marketing strategies. No, as we argue, the future lies in honest knowledge and authentic community, and those forward-thinking organizations with the savvy to realize this fact early on will, by our estimates, enjoy an unrivalled degree of consumer and brand loyalty. Let the power of the brand reside with the consumer.

By Jarrett Paschel, Ph.D.

while "world share" is becoming gradually more important. This is a trend that is not going away.

But when we talk about products and services the traditional criteria still apply. Strong product performance is the price of entry into commanding any space in any given lifestyle world, and none of the things we say about the importance of cultural branding has relevance for products that cannot compete on that basic level. But given strong performance in the following factors, cultural branding strategies will be essential for product differentiation in a dynamically changing marketplace.

1. quality threshold—While many brands attract consumers with the appeal of community and experience or their ability to contribute to a desirable identity, the quality of the product is also important. A poor product obviously has a negative impact on the brand's ability to attract new customers, while a great product attracts customers.

2. product reliability—Once the quality threshold is achieved, consistency of performance

over time and from purchase to purchase is essential. Products and brands must meet both in a consumer sensory as well as functional expectations.

3. product durability—Durability is the expected economic life of the product. Again, products and brands need to meet or exceed consumer expectations of longevity.

4. product serviceability—Serviceability is the ease of servicing the product if it needs repair. Thus, perceptions of product performance are affected by factors such as the speed, accuracy and care of product delivery and installation; the promptness, courtesy and helpfulness of customer service and training; and the quality of repair service and the time involved.

element 5: infrastructure sensibility

Related in a very important way to the element of products and services, another factor that both influences and is influenced by a lifestyle world must be considered, "infrastructure sensibility." It's the "presence" that a company possesses within a given lifestyle world in the sense of its brand identity as a company and the way it organizes its relationship with its customers.

General Motors has one kind of relationship with its customers; its satellite company Saturn has an entirely different kind of relationship. Harley-Davidson's relationship with its customers is legendary, or rather the relationship that Harley-Davidson customers have with the company borders on a cult. The most important point here is that the infrastructure sensibility is something that has to be facilitated, not engineered. Harley-Davidson did not engineer the cult that grew up around its motorcycles, but it was savvy enough to understand what was happening and found ways to cultivate and encourage and sustain its growth. Saturn's identity was deliberately kept independent from General Motors; however, the trust and brand identity that Saturn acquired came as an outgrowth of customer experience.

A company like Hostess, for instance, cannot expect its products to be accepted in, say, the wellness world, even if those products are by any objective standard healthier than other competing products in the wellness marketplace. Why? Because its infrastructure sensibility doesn't fit in the wellness lifestyle world. It could possibly create a satellite company with a different infrastructure sensibility, as GM did with Saturn, or acquire a smaller company with a grassroots connection as Coca-Cola did with Odwalla, but as a brand Hostess is simply not in and of itself ever a good fit in certain lifestyle worlds. And even if it were to create a satellite brand for the wellness market, it would have to follow the rules of brand development indigenous to that culture. Infrastructure sensibility cannot be grown, cultivated or forged in a customer-centric manner without a serious organizational re-tooling. Simply stating that the organization is "customer friendly,"

As part of a becoming a true cultural brand, it is imperative to be mindful of not just how consumers perceive your brand, but how they perceive the organization behind the brand. Be sensitive to what organizational decisions say to the consumer as part of the overall brand image, and the relationship these decisions have on the building of your brand's community, social context and experience. In order to build a consumer-sensitive organization you need to understand the alignment of consumer perception of your company:

? authority: Emphasize local autonomy and flexibility, replacing, where feasible, traditional, hierarchically oriented authority structures with "loose," horizontally aligned ties (i.e., loose coupling).

? uniformity: Wherever possible, avoid generalized, organizational philosophies as these tend to promote uniformity and consistency at the sake of individual initiative, creativity and spontaneity. Besides, if the organization is truly consumer driven, so-called "core competencies" will be forever changing to keep pace with ever-evolving consumer needs.

? efficiency: Abandon "organizational efficiency" initiatives. While efficiency may be desirable from an operations perspective, it doesn't necessarily have much to do with effectively meeting customer needs.

? predictability: Avoid "long range" forecasting and planning, for consumer sentiment is indeed ever shifting.

By Jarrett Paschel, Ph.D.

"brand driven" or "wellness-oriented" does nothing if the company is not organized as much. As we suggested in Part One, if the old mass market engineering techniques have had marginal practical effect even in the older more homogenous markets, they will have little if any effect in the new lifestyle marketplace.

The cultural brand starts with the consumer's perception of the company's credibility as a good fit with regard to the consumer's sensibility as it is shaped by the rules governing a particular lifestyle world. It's not just about product attributes. There has to be a match between the company's sensibility and the consumer's expectations while he or she is within a particular lifestyle world. Potentially, anyone can be a good match for, say, wellness, all they need to do is open themselves up to the world and let the consumer steer a truly consumer-centric organization. But first, one needs to consciously, and with deliberate effort (and care), create an organization that is in itself truly consumer-centric.

A true cultural brand can only be created when we decide to let go.

reflections on...

...the journey

As our work continues in understanding this "new" consumer, I'm constantly queried by the traditional marketplace as to the end-game: What's the group we need to target?...What's the size?...Who's the target market?...What are the demographics? When my response is to focus on the "journey," not the end game, eyebrows are raised. It's not that I'm implying these aren't appropriate questions, it's the simple fact that in a world where mores are still being formed and changed and behaviors have yet to be organized, these basic questions are secondary in our search for true consumer behavior. How many times have we fooled ourselves into believing that what consumers say they do on our attitudinal surveys, they actually do? Our efforts are far beyond that simplicity; and, it is that fact that perhaps many of these purists fail to understand the true nature of consumer change; life is messy...mine, yours and certainly the American consumer's.

We don't live in a world of specific patterns where, in the past, people fit more easily into homogenous groups—that much is clear. Our lives have changed because, most importantly, our world has changed. Whether it be in the enormous speed and diffusion of information, the traditional change in the infrastructures of our past or in our own search for a higher quality of life, the diversity of our complicated lives demands a different level of understanding—of ourselves and of the world in which we live, work and play. Or are we more like children in the candy store, where each child is in search of their individualized sweetness, affected by those around us but bound to our own individual taste?

American consumers are indeed on a journey, and we who try to understand them better should recognize that they have no developed and articulate end game. It's all about the trip...and what a trip it is. Those who pursue the end game are only generating answers to questions they themselves have created. Certainly in the minds of the consumers those questions are yet to be formulated. In the past ten years we have witnessed an enormous movement in the lives of American consumers, and that change is driven in part by a need for individualized regimes within the greater context of a community.

This is not easy to understand, and that's specifically why we have created an understanding of unique behavior from a world perspective where we can track movement and occasion, not individuals themselves. It's not a static marketplace we're living in. This is also why we strive to understand cultural components in relationship with changing behavior—people have and are changing the way they live, shop and buy. Why should we expect them to have all the answers in their lives when we don't? (At least most of us don't.)

The challenge today is in recognizing how these new consumers are integrating the past and the present, a culmination of unique behavior incorporating the new with the old, throwing the old way of choosing out the window and developing a whole new brand called "Me and My Family."

Let's have the courage to jump on the wagon, in the plane or whatever form of transportation we find appropriate and realize that understanding lies in the trip. Get your card punched and get ready, because around the bend is even more change, and still no end game is in sight. Hang on!

The epiphany here is in recognizing that we need to understand consumers in flux, consumers who seek and aspire to a different lifestyle. Boxing them into segments based upon the old vision doesn't give us the end game, it may only obstruct our ability to understand the journey, for even they don't know the final destination (if there is one at all).

What's even more complex is that their lives are filled with conflict: What about that runner who smokes? The supplement user who eats doughnuts? The organic produce shopper who doesn't recycle? The business exec who does yoga? These aren't so unusual. These are real people. They move on their own path and at their own speed, even as they profess a higher plane of decision, they behave on their own terms. And this is one thing that won't change.

Cultural brands will always allow consumers to move toward a destination they feel good about, both from a pragmatic use as well as an emotional attachment. As long as the brand invites consumers to participate on their own terms, not as an icon to a "better world," because they are concerned about their own world. The elements of a cultural brand that we talk about are those that can have a direct impact on an individual's life. Social Context. Community. Experience. Isn't that what a cultural brand is all about?

Isn't it the journey that is indeed the destination?

about
the hartman group

The Hartman Group, Inc., founded in 1989, is a full-service consulting and market research leader offering a wide range of services and products, with focus on the health and wellness arena. The company currently works out of offices in Bellevue, Washington.

Our experienced staff, with diverse, yet complementary backgrounds are experts in providing trade reports, syndicated studies, strategic consulting and customized research. This team has extensive knowledge and experience in marketing, business management, retail anthropology, sociology, nutrition, healthcare management, consumer economics and statistics.

In conjunction with our qualitative and quantitative research groups, The Hartman Group is consistently focused on uncovering key cultural linkages to major lines of force that are shaping and globalizing contemporary culture. These explorations linked to current Hartman Group consumer research are providing discoveries and insights on the attitudes and behaviors of what we term "core, mid-level and periphery consumers."

As consumer market researchers, our strength goes beyond just one-size-fits-all number tabulation and reporting. We understand today's consumer. We can provide your company the customized, one-on-one interface to give you the knowledge of who your consumer is and where they are going in the future.

contributors

harvey hartman—founder, chairman & CEO

An author, business school lecturer and former Fortune 500 senior executive, Harvey Hartman is a nationally recognized expert on American cultural change and the consumer activities that impact daily business products and services. He has co-authored a number of publications and books, including several major studies and research initiatives with a focus on the cultural and lifestyle changes of the consumer, such as *Natural Sensibility: A Study of America's Changing Culture & Lifestyle*. Harvey has authored two previous marketing texts, *Marketing in the Soul Age: Building Lifestyle Worlds* and *Marketing to the New Natural Consumer: Understanding Trends in Wellness*, focusing on the new changing dynamics of wellness and key forces driving the growth of the lifestyle marketplace. Harvey has consulted with major pharmaceutical, food and packaged goods companies in developing both strategic and tactical direction in this area. He has worked with the nonprofits, such as Mothers and Others for a Livable Planet, and has consulted to numerous government and NGO organizations such as the EPA, FDA, USDA, World Wildlife Fund, Co-op America and The Food Alliance.

jarrett paschel, PhD—retail sociologist

Jarrett Paschel's research interests are keenly focused at the intersection of culture, economy and society, with particular emphasis on consumer behavior in the retail arena. In addition to his ongoing research activities at The Hartman Group, he is currently at work on a manuscript examining non-rational foundations to marketplace behavior, influenced in part by little-used threads from metaphysics and epistemology. Most recently he served as a research fellow at the Center for Study of Myth and Ritual in the American Family at Emory University, with previous experience as a restaurant critic, wine educator, freelance writer and university instructor.

jack whelan—director, trends group

Jack Whelan, with a Master of Arts and Religion from Yale University, is the Director of the Trends Group with The Hartman Group. He was senior editor at The Seabury Press in New York and developmental editor at the University of Washington Press. Jack also lectures in communications at the University of Washington Business School. In addition to several articles that have appeared in Hartman Group publications, he has published "American Soul" in *The Noetic Science Review*, Spring 1998.

david moore, PhD—statistical methods

David Moore oversees the statistical analysis of consumer attitudes and behaviors. He has over ten years of experience in statistical consulting and applied research, including sampling, multivariate analysis, event history modeling and demographic methods. His research interests include investigating lifestyle and cultural influences on the development of cardiovascular disease, and modeling changes in individual behavior over the life-course.

michelle barry, PhD—vice president, qualitative research

Michelle Barry has extensive experience in the dietary supplement, natural products and healthcare industries. Her previous experience includes conventional healthcare management, physician's assistant and nutritional advisor for an alternative care facility in Seattle, Washington. Michelle has recently completed her Ph.D. in medical anthropology at the University of Washington.

jerry savage—ethnographic analyst

Prior to joining The Hartman Group, Jerry conducted empirical research on the New Age movement and the market for New Age products. Currently, his interests include the culture of wellness, the nature of the individual and triangular (multi-method) research designs.

joelle chizmar—editor & director of publications

Joelle Chizmar directs all publication projects for The Hartman Group, including editorial content and calendars. She is also the editor of *N\sight Magazine*, The Hartman Group's biannual publication and *HartBeat*, The Hartman Group's online newsletter. Joelle also directs all Hartman Group's web communication projects, including Hartman Interactive, The Hartman Group's online panel and interactive dialogue system. Her previous experience includes working as an English educator in public schools, focusing on writing instruction and interactive learning, and as a program manager for various non-profit, educational programs.

other books by harvey hartman
& the hartman group

marketing in the soul age:
building lifestyle worlds, 2001
Showcasing our innovative perspective on consumer insights and understanding, this publication analyzes the reasons for the shattering of the post-World War II mass market and prescribes an approach for developing strategies to reach consumers in the new lifestyle marketplace, outlining the Hartman Model and the "world perspective."

destination wellness:
the consumer, the store, the brand, the future, 2000
This cutting-edge compilation aids the existing conventional supermarket industry and those businesses newly interested in the health and wellness category in understanding current market dynamics and strategic requirements to maximize wellness shopping in the traditional grocery setting.

marketing to the new natural consumer:
understanding trends in wellness, 1999
This comprehensive text looks at the evolving natural products marketplace, including a history of the natural and organic industry, an analysis of who the "new natural consumer" is, an exploration of America's changing culture and lifestyle, and marketing implications for building natural brands in the wellness category.

These and other Hartman Group reports and publications can be found at www.hartman-group.com.